CLASSIC GUITAR CONSTRUCTION

CLASSIC GUITAR CONSTRUCTION

Diagrams, photographs, and step-by-step instructions / IRVING SLOANE

E. P. DUTTON & CO., INC. *New York*

Library of Congress Catalog Card Number:
66-14680

FIRST EDITION

ACKNOWLEDGMENTS

The guitar-building methods described in this book are the result of ten years of inquiry, surmise, and experience. In this process I received initial encouragement from Manuel Velazquez and Gene Villa-Lobos. More recently, I have benefited from the valuable experience of José Rubio, a luthier with an impressive and well-deserved reputation. Both he and his wife, Nest, gave generously of their time and interest.

Law Zabriskie contributed wise counsel about wood, and good friend Wentworth Schofield computed the accurate fretting scale.

The fine old guitars pictured in the book appear through the courtesy of Otto Winkler, George Giusti, Anita Sheer, and Felipe Gayo.

Vladimir Bobri and Professor Michael Kasha provided encouragement and editorial assistance.

I sincerely thank them all.

Irving Sloane

For Peter Reinhardt

Contents

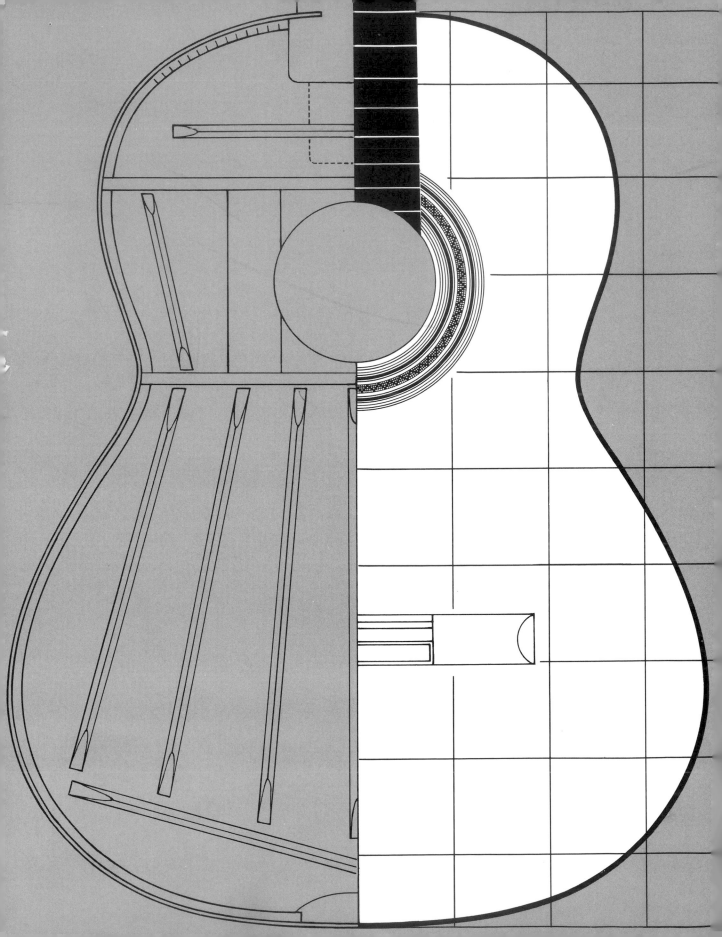

Introduction

Spain is the ancestral home of the classic guitar. The world's greatest guitars have come from the workbenches of Spanish luthiers and Spanish composers have contributed a rich literature for this favored instrument. Although the evolution of the medieval guitar into its modern counterpart took place in Spain, the guitar actually came to Spain from across the Mediterranean to the south.

Early in the eighth century A.D., dark-skinned Moors from North Africa overran the Iberian peninsula and dominated Spain for almost eight hundred years. During the eleventh and twelfth centuries, successive waves of Moorish invasions brought to Spain large numbers of skilled artisans who settled in the great cities of Andalusia—Córdoba, Granada, Seville. Moslem architects built the Alhambra and Moorish troubadors brought their music and musical instruments to their new homeland. In addition to *al' ud,* Arabic precursor of the lute, they brought other stringed instruments—including a form of the guitar. This early guitar had the characteristic guitar outline but was smaller than the modern guitar and had upper and lower bouts of nearly equal size. It held four strings and was played with a plectrum.

Instrument-makers set up shop and by the end of the thirteenth century instrument-making was a refined art in Andalusia. Moorish luthiers began the long tradition that culminated in the triumphant work of Antonio de Torres Jurado in the mid-nineteenth century.

Torres, an obscure Spanish carpenter, became intrigued with the tonal possibilities of the guitar. His experiments led to important innovations that gave the guitar unprecedented brilliance and power. Working with superb artistry he enlarged the sound chest, refined the outline, fixed the string length at 650 millimeters, and devised a novel system of bracing the sound board to enhance tone. Torres'

Fig. 1   Basic Torres pattern (exactly ½ size)

Fig. 2   TORRES' DEVELOPMENT OF MODERN GUITAR

José Pernas, 1843
(taught Torres guitar-making
principles)

Torres, 1854

Torres, 1857

"La Leona"
Torres, 1858

Torres, 1866

Torres, 1888

(Courtesy Winkler Collection)

contributions passed to Vicente Arias and Manuel Ramirez, who in turn taught Enrique Garcia, Santos Hernandez, Domingo Esteso, and others—all luthiers of the first rank.

A sensitive regard for the guitar's design as well as tonal possibilities has been a singular virtue of Spanish guitar-making. The simple elegance of proportion and detail—the profile of the head, the sound-hole mosaic inlay, the sculptured heel—attest to an innate sensitivity to form and design. The beauty of Spanish guitars is unsurpassed.

Today, millions of music lovers are captivated by the vibrant charm and intimacy of the classic guitar. Virtuoso performers have brought to recording and concert hall its splendid repertoire and students flock to the guitar.

Guitar sales are soaring as factories in the United States and abroad work at top speed to fill the demand. Unfortunately, fine guitars cannot be made at top speed and mediocrity is the rule. In Spain, $120 will buy a guitar of a quality that cannot be duplicated in the United States at any price except by a few private luthiers. Hand-made guitars start at about $500.

For the person accustomed to playing a factory model, a guitar from the hand of a skilled luthier is always a revelation. The tone, action, craftsmanship, and finish make playing such an instrument a unique pleasure. Inferior guitars are difficult to play.

Nevertheless, great quantities of guitars are sold at disproportionately high prices despite their almost uniform lack of those qualities that characterize a well-made classic guitar. The sheer economics and mechanics of mass production and mass distribution preclude the manufacture of superior instruments in accordance with classic principles. Apart from this, what is more grievously lacking is the judgment and skill of a single man—one who knows, for instance, that the density of a given

set of rosewood sides and back calls for a top of a certain temper and thickness and perhaps a change in the bracing.

The classic guitar is a delicate equation painstakingly conceived to produce a brilliant, balanced tone over its entire playable range. The story of the great guitar-makers is the story of the quest for this perfection. There are no secrets hidden away that will unlock the door to success. The "secret" of the men who have succeeded in mastering this equation is simply the skill born of infinite patience and the knowledge born of experience.

Construction Theory

Taking the violin as a point of departure, certain observations may be made about guitar construction.

The violin is a shallow, comparatively small wooden box "tuned" to produce the strong sonorities of a bow drawn across its strings; dimensions, thicknesses, and volume of enclosed air are carefully regulated to accomplish this end. Increasing the volume of air enclosed in the carcass of a bowed instrument (as progressively in the viola, cello, and double bass) increases the bass resonance. The same is true of the guitar. Larger, deeper guitars accentuate and deepen the bass response; shallow guitars accentuate the treble end of the scale and also suffer a reduction in volume or loudness.

A properly constructed guitar has a vibrant, well-braced body and a sound board especially designed to vibrate. Guitars with tops that cannot vibrate produce a muffled, insubstantial sound. Bracing and thickness of the top must be carefully adjusted to insure that the top vibrates in a manner that will produce a clear, singing tone.

A guitar made with thin back and sides tends to be louder than a guitar made of thicker

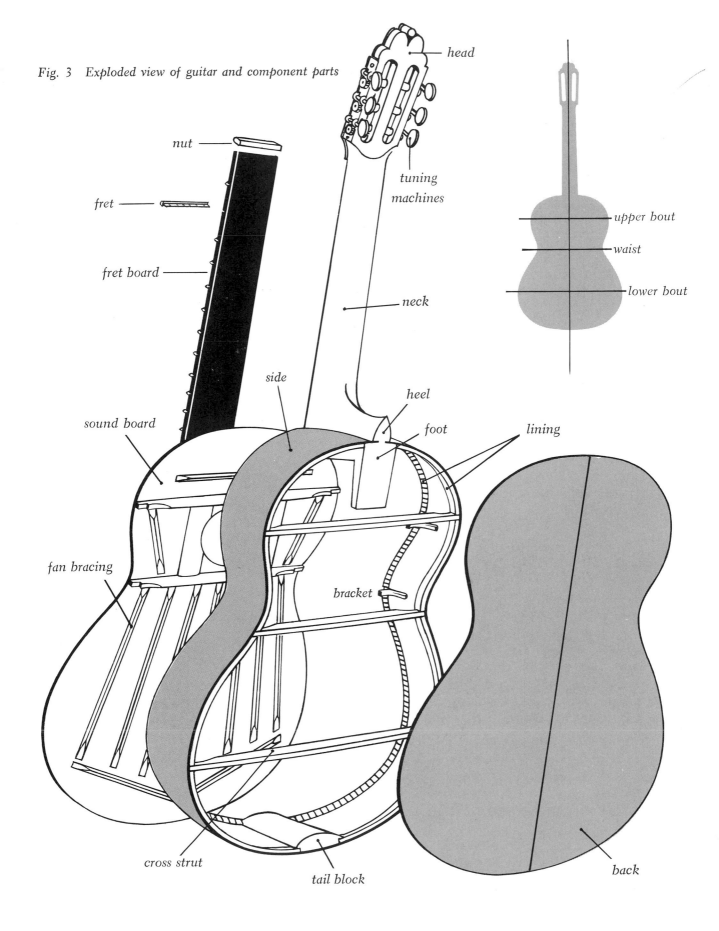

Fig. 3 Exploded view of guitar and component parts

head

nut

fret

fret board

tuning machines

neck

side

heel

foot

lining

sound board

fan bracing

bracket

upper bout

waist

lower bout

cross strut

tail block

back

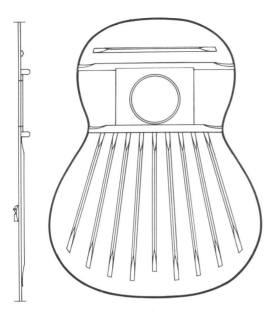

Fig. 4   Traditional fan bracing

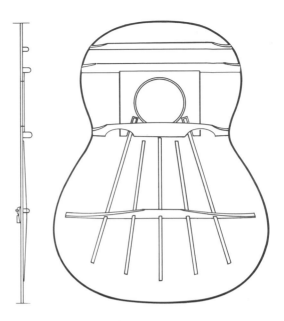

Fig. 5   Bouchet system

wood. A "thin" guitar also produces disturbing overtones and dissonances unless securely and strategically braced.

The guitar-maker's basic job, then, is to make a guitar thin enough to produce adequate volume, stable enough to preclude harmonic difficulties, and with a top that will flex properly to lend body and presence to the sound.

This golden mean is what the luthier strives for; how to achieve it cannot be reduced to a pat formula. A systematic study of the great makers' guitars reveals subtle changes in thicknesses and dimensions from one instrument to the next. No two are the same. This might be thought accidental were it not for the fact that nothing would have been more simple for craftsmen of the stature of Ramirez and Hernandez than to continually produce the same pattern. It may also explain why they chose to work without molds, which gave them unlimited freedom to alter the outline, a facility restricted by the use of a mold.

They constantly made slight changes, using their skill and judgment to unlock the combination that would liberate the tonal eloquence they sought.

Fan Bracing

The slender spruce braces glued to the under side of the sound board are an essential element in tone production. Their size and pattern of distribution greatly affect the quality of sound produced.

The large circular area of the sound board encompassed by the lower bouts is a diaphragm; bracing serves to discipline the movement of this surface—an unbraced sound board is free to "flap" in an uncontrolled manner.

Movement of the sound board results from the vibrations of sound waves entering the sound hole and the transmission of string vibrations to the bridge, which in turn transmits

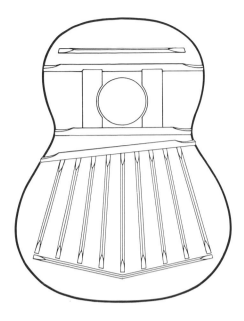

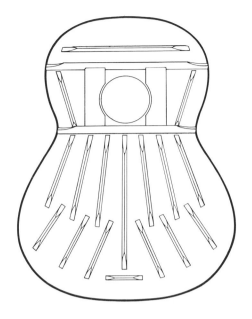

Fig. 6   *Transverse bar*   Fig. 7   *Broken fan (author)*

them to the sound board. This ultrarapid rise and fall of the resonating diaphragm sets air in motion in the sound chest, amplifying and increasing the duration of sound waves. This amplitude gives body and power to the tone of a guitar.

Patterns of bracing in guitar construction are so numerous as to suggest that this has been a provocative area for experimentation. The majority are designed to promote the movement of sound vibrations across the diaphragm like the effect of a stone dropped in the center of a pond; concentric circles of sound vibrations ripple out from the bridge, meeting less and less resistance as they reach the diaphragm perimeter.

The basic Torres bracing pattern is still the most widely accepted design. However, a French guitar-maker, Robert Bouchet, has developed a system of bracing which has produced some superb guitars (Fig. 5). Bouchet's design extends the vibrating surface

up toward the sound hole and employs a central fan arrangement connected to an arched crosspiece positioned directly under the bridge saddle. Because of the tricky fitting of the fan through the arched crosspiece, this design is difficult to make. The results have nevertheless been most impressive, and craftsmen of advanced skill will find this bracing method a rewarding challenge.

The bracing around the sound hole serves to prevent "flutter"—movement of the sound-hole edges that might distort sound waves entering the body.

The crossbrace in back of the large strut at the top exists to prevent cracks in the top along each side of the fret board. The denser fret board expands and contracts at a different rate than the softer, thinner spruce, sometimes causing cracks.

All bracing arrangements reinforce the top and help modify dimensional movement caused by changes in atmospheric moisture.

Humidity

Dampness is the enemy of all stringed instruments, particularly the guitar.

If dampness enters wood, the wood swells. In a drier environment the moisture leaves the wood and the wood shrinks to its former size. This cycle of dampness and drying is fairly normal, and a guitar can tolerate these changes if they are gradual and not extreme.

A guitar built in an atmosphere where the relative humidity level is about 65 per cent most of the time will survive well in that atmosphere. If it is removed abruptly to a relative-humidity level of 20 it will surely crack after enough moisture has been lost. If a guitar is built at a humidity level of 35, acclimated to a 65 per cent humidity level, and then removed to a humidity situation of 20, it may still crack—but the probability is greatly reduced.

If possible, a guitar should be assembled in an atmosphere containing less moisture than the atmosphere in which it will finally consistently be. As a general rule, it is best to build guitars in a dry environment because swelling is less of a hazard than shrinkage.

The critical surfaces for contraction and expansion in a guitar are the top and back. The end grain (easiest point of entry for atmospheric moisture) is sealed off by the purfling. Absorption of moisture is further retarded by the varnish or other protective finish. If the guitar is well braced and carefully constructed, the problem of swelling is not great. The most scrupulous craftsmanship, however, counts for little in the face of a precipitous loss of moisture and the resultant deformation of wood.

Before you proceed with plans to build a guitar, find out from the local weather bureau the mean annual averages for high and low humidity in your area. If the mean average high is 79 and the low is 28, the mean annual average relative humidity in your area is 53.5 per cent. You should assemble your guitar in an atmosphere that does not exceed this humidity level.

Work in a basement workshop must be done only when the basement is dry—usually during the winter months when the furnace dries the air. To extend the working season into the warmer, more humid months, the air in the workshop must be dehumidified. This can be accomplished with an electric dehumidifier, an automatic device that condenses moisture from the atmosphere. An air conditioner also helps control humidity.

A good hygrometer (a device for measuring percentage of relative humidity) is an important workshop investment. Hang it on a wall away from doors and windows.

Freshly purchased wood should be kept under a weighted board until acclimated to workshop atmosphere, normally a few weeks. After the wood reaches equilibrium with the surrounding atmosphere it may be stacked on a high shelf and turned over at intervals.

Guitars—complete or incomplete—must not be stored near sources of heat or moisture. Never leave a guitar in a closed case where the sun's rays can "cook" it. If you do not take your guitar with you during summer vacations, loosen strings and store the instrument in the coolest, driest part of the house.

Always remember that a guitar is a fragile, taut ensemble of wood and strings.

Fig. 8   Hygrometer

Wood and Materials

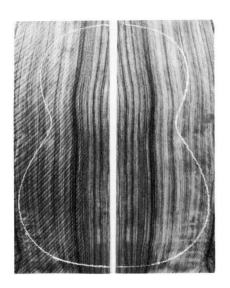

Fig. 9   Brazilian rosewood back

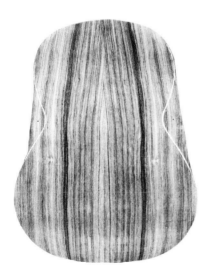

The finest wood for making a classical guitar is Brazilian rosewood, a dense, resinous wood that ranges in color from light tan to deep chocolate brown. Unfortunately, this wood is in short supply and costly. East Indian rosewood is an excellent alternate but maple, birch, pear, mahogany and other woods have also been used in the construction of fine guitars. Almost without exception, however, Brazilian rosewood remains first choice among professional guitar-makers.

The flamenco guitar, a variant of the classic guitar, is usually made of Spanish cypress, a light, aromatic blond wood native to Spain. This wood is believed to impart to flamenco guitars their characteristic warmth. Each kind of wood imparts its own subtle tonal coloration to a guitar.

For beauty and ease of handling, avoid highly figured wood. Straight-grain wood has a simplicity that esthetically complements the graceful contours of the classic guitar.

Dark rosewood is preferred to lighter shades because it shows light inlay to advantage. Tradition also dictates the use of darker wood; more important, there is an undeniable richness in the handsome austerity of a deep-brown finish. Rough-sawn rosewood, incidentally, appears deceptively lighter than its finished appearance.

Wood with such obvious defects as cracks, knots, pinholes, black pitch markings, and unsightly color variations should not be used. The pieces for the two sides should be perfectly flat. Sides that are warped diagonally will not be straightened by the forming process. The back is one piece of wood sliced so that both halves will make a symmetrical design when butted (Fig. 9). The sides should also be symmetrical and should match the color and grain of the back.

In apportioning the investment for guitar

materials, the sound board comes first. It is the most important element in the guitar. Torres built a guitar with back and sides of papier-mâché to demonstrate the key role of the top in tone production. (Guitarists who played this instrument said it possessed an extraordinary tone.)

Just where or how spruce was discovered to have acoustic properties is a mystery buried in the past, but the oldest surviving stringed instruments prove that ancient instrument-makers knew the natural resonating quality of spruce.

The best-quality spruce comes from near the timber line of the mountains of central Europe. Blanks for sound boards are cut from radially sawn lumber. Grain pattern runs from closely spaced heartwood to more open-grained sap-wood.

Sound boards are selected by grain, temper (resilience), and resonance. A good top is seasoned, unblemished, and close-grained. Annular divisions should run about twelve to sixteen per inch. Where the grain widens at the outer edges the increase should be gradual. End grain should be almost vertical; if it is badly slanted it means the wood was cut tangentially and is more likely to warp. A characteristic of the best spruce tone wood is a cross-grain "silk" pattern observable in the finest guitars.

Flexing the board will reveal its resilience. It should be fairly stiff with only a slight amount of spring. Generally, stiffer boards will give a brighter edge to the sound than softer, more flexible boards. Very soft boards that bend easily are not used.

Although the most reliable index for selecting tops is visual, the resonating quality may be judged by lightly grasping the upper edge of one of the halves and gently rapping it with the knuckles of the free hand. Even an inexperienced person can detect differences in resonance by listening carefully. A good, dry sound board has a certain "live" tone while a poor one will have a relatively dead response. As the wood is worked to the appropriate thinness, thumping produces a brighter, more noticeable ring.

Finger boards or fret boards are made of ebony or rosewood. Ebony is always used on guitars of high quality because of its durability, lack of grain, and the elegant contrast it makes with nickel-silver frets. It is almost impossible to find completely jet-black ebony; streaks or veinings of gray are common. If these marks are unobtrusive they will eventually disappear, darkened by the oil and perspiration of the player's hand. If they are prominent enough to require staining, a black stain from Germany (*Ebonholzbeize*) is good. Both ends of ebony finger boards usually come sealed with paraffin or shellac to keep moisture from seeping into the end grain and warping the board. A warped finger board must be discarded.

Struts and bracing for the top are made of straight-grain clear Sitka spruce, a light, strong wood stocked by lumber yards that sell boat lumber. The narrow fan bracing can sometimes be rescued from the waste portion of the sound board by judicious jigsawing. Do not use basswood for strutting or bracing the top.

Honduras mahogany is used for the cross struts on rosewood backs, Sitka spruce or maple on maple backs.

The neck is made of straight-grain Honduras mahogany, a strong, exceptionally stable wood that ranges in color from a yellowish to a reddish tan. Texture is mellow and easily worked.

Lining is usually basswood (linden), sometimes Honduras mahogany.

All guitar wood must be kept in the workroom atmosphere for several weeks before you begin construction.

Tuning machines are sold in matched sets.

Fig. 10 Superior quality tuning machine

Prices range widely, as does quality. When purchasing machines, check the shafts for alignment. Do not buy a set with a bent shaft or faceplate. Check for cracked rollers and damaged buttons. Turn each button. The shaft should start turning as soon as the button is turned. If the button turns a bit before engaging the gear, the gear is misaligned.

Wooden pegs for flamenco guitars are sold as viola pegs by violin supply houses and are available in rosewood and ebony.

The bridge is fashioned from a billet of straight-grain rosewood. Bone and ivory are sold by guitar supply houses for the nut, bridge saddle, and bridge trim. Ivory is much more expensive than bone. It stays white longer and ages more handsomely than bone, which often acquires a greasy appearance. Ivory is universally preferred by luthiers for expensive instruments.

LIST OF MATERIALS

Sound board: 2 pieces spruce $7\frac{1}{2}'' \times 20''$

Back: 2 pieces rosewood or maple, $7\frac{1}{2}'' \times 20''$

Sides: 2 pieces rosewood or maple, cut from same flitch as back, $4'' \times 32''$

Neck: 1 piece of Honduras mahogany (see pg. 44 for dimensions)
1 piece each holly veneer and rosewood ($\frac{1}{16}''$ thick), $4'' \times 8''$

Tail block: 1 piece mahogany or basswood, $1'' \times 3'' \times 4''$

Linings: 2 pieces shaped for kerfing, 2 pieces flat, $\frac{5}{32}'' \times \frac{5}{8}'' \times 30''$

Cross struts (sound board): 2 pieces Sitka spruce, $1\frac{1}{32}'' \times \frac{5}{8}'' \times 12''$

Rosette: 1 mosaic inlay, bought or made (see pg. 80)

Cross struts (back): 3 pieces mahogany (rosewood guitar) or 3 pieces maple (maple guitar), $1\frac{1}{32}'' \times \frac{5}{8}'' \times 15''$

Cross-grain bracing for back: $\frac{1}{16}'' \times \frac{1}{2}'' \times 16''$ mahogany

Bracing: 11 pieces Sitka spruce, $\frac{3}{16}'' \times \frac{1}{4}'' \times 9''$

Bridge: 1 piece rosewood, $\frac{1}{2}'' \times 1\frac{1}{4}'' \times 8''$

Fret board: 1 piece ebony or rosewood, $\frac{1}{4}'' \times 2\frac{3}{4}'' \times 18\frac{1}{2}''$

Bridge saddle and nut: ivory or bone

Inlay for back: 1 piece rosewood veneer strip, $\frac{1}{8}'' \times 20''$ (maple guitar)
1 piece maple veneer strip, $\frac{1}{8}'' \times 20''$ (rosewood guitar)

Purfling: 2 pieces $\frac{3}{16}''$ black-white-black (fine)
4 pieces $\frac{3}{16}''$ black-white
4 pieces $\frac{3}{16}''$ rosewood veneer
4 pieces $\frac{1}{8}''$ rosewood veneer
4 pieces $\frac{1}{16}''$ black-white side fillet
(Purfling is usually sold in $36''$ lengths. It is wise to buy two extra of each for safety. If the side fillet is omitted, buy eight pieces of the $\frac{3}{16}''$ rosewood instead of four.)

Tuning machines: 1 set with screws for faceplate holes

German silver *fret wire* with studded tang, $48''$.

NOTE. The beginning guitar-maker should make his first guitar of plain, unfigured maple and omit the side fillets. Unfigured maple is inexpensive and will make a beautiful guitar. The side fillets are attractive but entail a good bit of effort. Advanced craftsmen will have no problem.

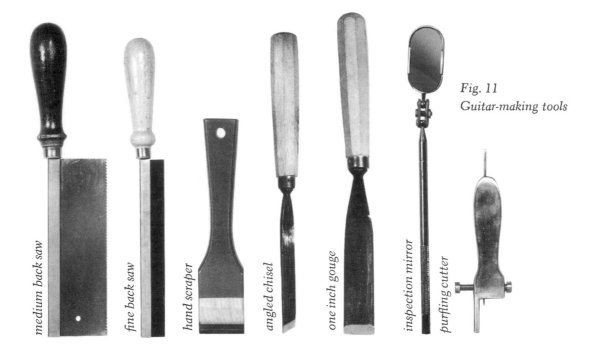

medium back saw   fine back saw   hand scraper   angled chisel   one inch gouge   inspection mirror   purfling cutter

Fig. 11
Guitar-making tools

Tools

Deep-throat clamps (page 31) and a purfling cutter (page 33) are the only special tools required for guitar-making. In addition, you will need these ordinary tools:

Fine back saw, ¾″ blade width

Medium back saw, 2″ blade width (for sawing fret grooves)

Jig or coping saw

½″ and 1″ gouges

1⁄16″, ¼″, and ½″ chisels

5⁄8″ angled chisel (for shaping braces)

Hand scrapers

3″ × 5″ steel scraper blade and steel burnisher

Adjustable block plane or smoothing plane

Wire nippers

36″ metal straightedge

6″ circle cutter

Hand or power drill with 5⁄8″, 13⁄32″, and 1⁄16″ bits

Assorted clamps

Flexible inspection mirror

If you own power tools—radial or bench saw, jigsaw, band saw, and drill press—you will save time but fine guitars can be made without any power equipment. An inexperienced craftsman, however, will have trouble drilling accurate holes for the tuning machines and string holes in the bridge without a drill press.

A small routing machine, if available, will quickly clean purfling ledges after the top outlines have been cut with the purfling tool. The straight, fluted router bit is adjusted for the purfling depth.

Cutting tools must be kept at razor sharpness for maximum working efficiency. You will need a medium and rough grit combination carborundum stone and a hard Arkansas stone to keep tool edges keen.

Hold the cutting bevel of the tool against the rough and then the medium grit stone and hone with a small circular motion. Keep the surface well oiled to prevent metal filings from clogging the surface of the stone. When the bevel is flat and uniform, shift to the Arkansas stone. Hone in the same manner until all scratches made by the medium grit stone are gone, leaving the bevel shiny-smooth. Turn the blade over and hold it flat against the stone. Remove the burr by moving the blade sideways an inch once or twice. Test the blade for sharpness on a scrap piece of wood. Repeat the fine honing step if necessary until the blade cuts smoothly and easily.

Gouges are sharpened with a sweeping, rolling motion as they are passed over the stone. The burr on the inner edge is removed with a wedge-shaped roundnosed slipstone.

Drawing an edge on a steel-scraper blade is a tricky job that requires practice. The long edges must be honed dead flat and square by sliding the blade over the stone, using a wooden support to keep it perfectly vertical (Fig. 12). The blade is then laid on its side and honed until the edge is knife-edge square. Clamp the blade in a vise with the cutting edge up. Oil the edge liberally and draw a steel burnisher (Stanley) over the edge. Make three or four passes exerting uniform pressure with the burnisher held first at 90 degrees. Increase the angle until the last pass is made at an angle of about 85 degrees, turning the edge over in a slight hook (Fig. 13).

Sanding sticks are easy to make, more efficient and less harsh than steel files, and make the most efficient use of sandpaper. Three sticks covered with rough, medium, and medium-fine grit aluminum oxide paper will suffice for making one guitar. Sticks should be about 3⁄8″ × 1¾″ × 18″ for most comfortable use and can be reused by covering with fresh sandpaper.

Fig. 12   Squaring scraper blade edge

Fig. 13   Drawing edge into hook with burnisher

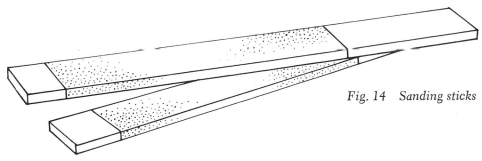

Fig. 14   Sanding sticks

Construction Forms

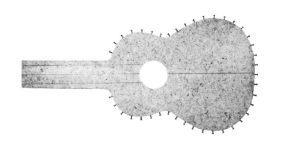

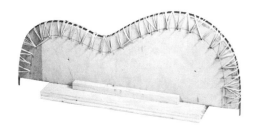

Fig. 15   Basic forms

Several forms are necessary to build a guitar: a mold, a bending form, two purfling forms, and a work board. The work board serves as a jig for gluing back and top to sides and also as a general form for holding the guitar while working on it.

The *mold* is the basic form in which sides and neck are assembled. It is possible to build a guitar without a mold, but one is necessary for the mode of construction described in this book. It is a convenient means of insuring symmetry in the important first stages of construction. The top and back are assembled outside the mold. A later section details an alternate method of construction in which the mold is employed throughout the entire construction process; see page 66.

The *bending form* is a contoured device for holding and fixing the shape of the sides.

Purfling forms are used to assemble decorative strips of edge banding into a laminated, shaped member ready for installation as a single unit. These forms are not assembled until the carcass of the guitar is complete.

A lumber sandwich of several boards—each measuring 10″ × 24″—yields the principal elements of these basic forms plus a template. The waste portion of the sandwich is used as a squeeze jig to correct imperfectly bent sides.

The sandwich is made up of:

> 2 pieces ¾″ × 10″ × 24″ plywood
> 2 pieces 1¾″ × 10″ × 24″ lumber core (or 4 pieces of 5⁄4″ × 10″ × 24″ lumber)
> 1 piece ⅛″ × 10″ × 24″ Masonite (template)

This lumber can often be found in the bargain bin at local lumber yards. Stacked, the depth of the sandwich is approximately 5″.

Project the half-pattern of the guitar (Fig. 1) twice size and draw it onto the top of the sandwich. Spend enough time to insure maximum fidelity to the original pattern. When this has been neatly penciled in, draw another line 1½" outside the first outline. This line is the outside of the mold. Drill pilot holes to avoid splitting and nail ten-penny nails through the top and back of the sandwich to hold it together securely while it is being band sawed. Keep nails well clear of the two penciled outlines the band saw will follow.

Sand smooth the long side of the sandwich on which the guitar pattern is centered. Take the sandwich to a yard that handles millwork, or to a cabinetmaker, for band sawing. The sawing of the inner outline must be executed in one continuous cut. Diameter of the band-saw blade should be ¼" to negotiate the curve at the waist comfortably.

Glue the waste portion together and set it aside. Sort the several pieces that will comprise the layered halves of the mold. Lay them out on the workbench to make sure they are properly stacked to form a continuous, symmetrical mold in the shape of a guitar. Glue the sections of each half separately, using white glue. When both halves are glued, align them and clamp them in a vise with their inner face up. Sand the end faces and the inner contour smooth. Fill all holes with wood putty. Unclamp and reverse the sides on the workbench and check the fit of the two end faces. Sand

them to butt tightly and glue. A long clamp across the waist will hold the ends together during gluing.

When dry, draw a line 1⅞" from each side of the center joint at the top of the mold. Drill a ⅝" hole in the center of each of these lines. Saw down through the lines bisecting the drill holes, releasing the center piece—the gate.

Cut two 2½" lengths of ⅝" dowel, glue them into the drill grooves in the ends of the mold, and replace the gate. The dowels do *not* glue to the gate. With the gate in place, apply a clamp across the waist to press the dowels into their grooves during gluing. When dry, sand the dowels and gate grooves to an easy fit; a close fit is unnecessary.

Draw a bold, clean line down the center of a ¾" × 18" × 33" pressed wood or plywood board. This board is the mold base. With gate still in place, align the mold on the center line, its bottom edge flush with the bottom of the board. Trace both inner and outer contours of the mold onto the board. Draw on either side of the center line the parallel lines which serve as a guide for aligning the neck. Draw the circles to be removed with a circle cutter. They lighten the weight of the mold and provide handy exits for debris that collects inside.

Position the mold on the cutout base and clamp the two together. Drill pilot holes in the back for 1½" flat-head screws. Countersink the holes and unclamp. Apply a liberal coat of Titebond or white glue to the bottom of the mold and glue it in place on the base. Fasten the screws and clean off all excess glue.

In subsequent illustrations, one of the molds has a plastic liner laminated to the inner face, a useful device for concealing a badly flawed inner wall. A clear coat of shellac or varnish will fix the pencil lines and preserve the completed form.

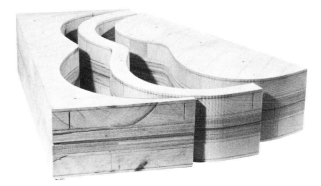

Fig. 16 Lumber sandwich yields principal elements of forms

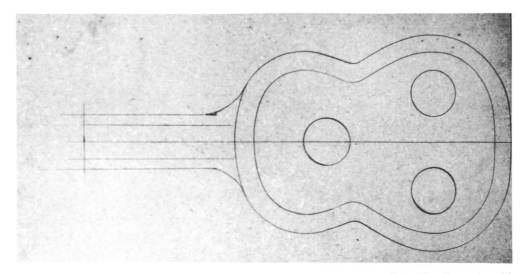

Fig. 17   *Base of mold*

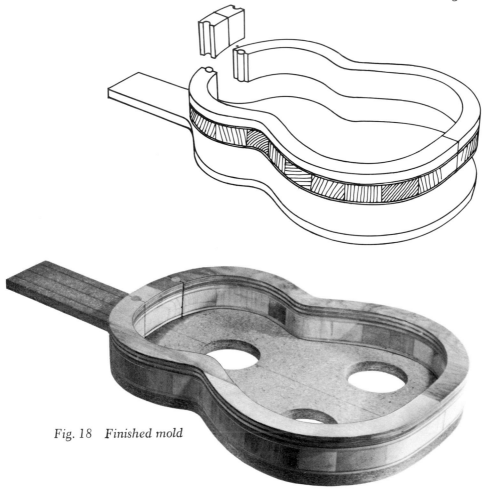

Fig. 18   *Finished mold*

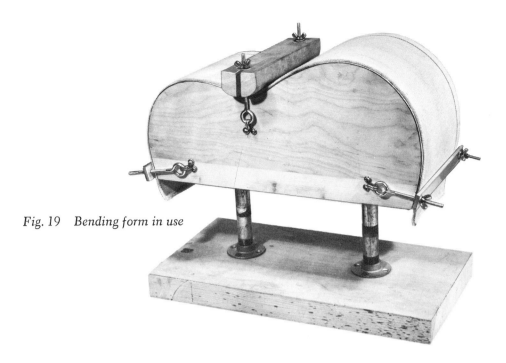

Fig. 19   Bending form in use

Bending Form

These materials are necessary to build the bending form:

> Six ¼" × 4" threaded eye bolts with washers and wing nuts
> Six 1¼" eye screws
> 9" × 32" sheet of medium-gauge aluminum, zinc, or tin
> Two 1" × 6" pipe, threaded both ends
> Four threaded pipe collars
> 9" × 36" heavy canvas
> Two ¼" × 1" × 10½" aluminum straps
> 1¾" × 10" × 20" lumber-core base or 2" × 10" × 20" lumber
> 2" × 4" × 11" lumber for waist block
> 2" × 10" × 20" lumber for the base

The bending form is shaped into an exaggerated representation of the actual guitar contour to compensate for springback. Resaw and sand the two sides to the pattern of Fig. 20.

Saw the 2" × 10" × 20" piece of lumber for the bottom of the form to a width of 9".

Glue the sides to this plank. Saw and sand the ends of the plank to conform to the shape of the sides.

Fasten the collars to the bottom of the plank. Screw in pipes and screw on the bottom collars. Screw the bottom collars into the base.

Bend the metal sheet to the shape of the guitar and drill ³⁄₁₆" holes at 2" intervals along both edges. Countersink the holes and screw in ¾" screws (rustproof).

Position the eye screws on both sides of the form, then drill pilot holes and screw them in. Force open the large eye on the eye bolts and hook them onto the small eye screws. Close the large eye so it cannot slip out. (The small fixtures used to hold the eye bolts in the illustration were bought in a marine-hardware supply house. Small eye screws are a more generally available substitute and work just as well.)

Drill ¼" holes in the two metal straps that clamp the ends. Round off the bottom of the 11" piece of 2" × 4" until it fits the incurved waist. Rough out the shape with plane and rasp. Finish with sandpaper. Saw the end slots that engage the side bolts.

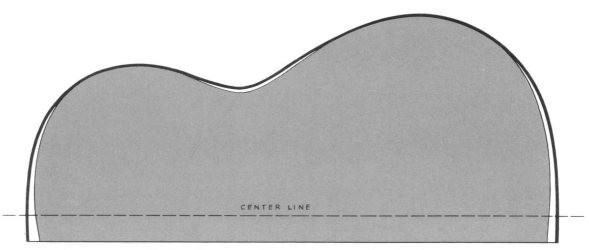

CENTER LINE

Fig. 20   Pattern modification for sides of bending form

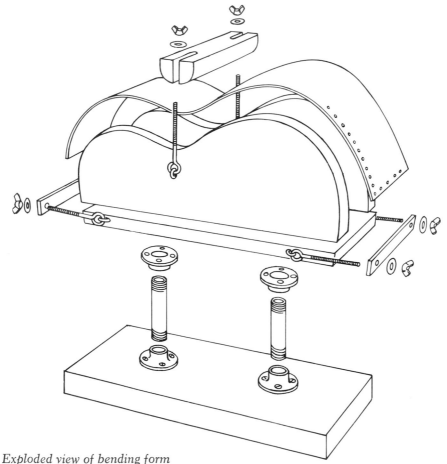

Fig. 21   Exploded view of bending form

Work Board

The work board is cut from a ¾″ × 16″ × 34″ piece of pressed wood. Jigsaw the shape to the pattern (Fig. 22) and sand the outline smooth. Insert 1″ round-head rustproof screws all around the perimeter of the body, spaced 1½″ apart. Screw them in until the thread is buried and only the smooth shank is left. Rubber bands are looped around these screws and laced back and forth across the body of the guitar to exert pressure while the top and back are glued on. A one-pound box of ⅝″ × 7″ rubber bands will provide an adequate supply for lacing.

For general use clamp the work board to the edge of a workbench so that the body projects out from the bench. The guitar can be secured to the form by a clamp at the neck or a number of rubber bands stretched across the body.

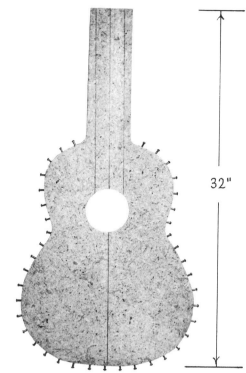

Fig. 22   Work board is cut slightly larger than actual guitar shape

Fig. 23   Work board in use as gluing jig

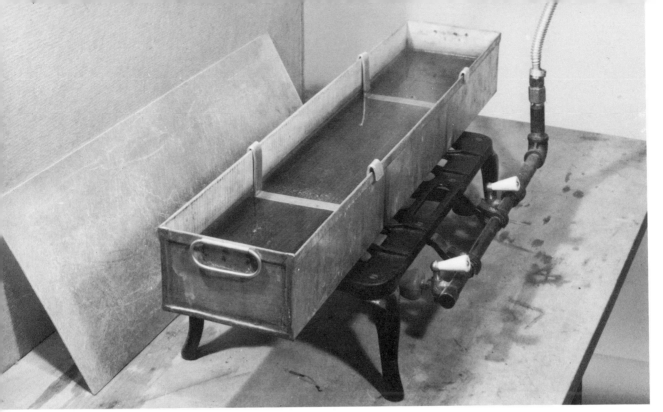

Fig. 24   Boiling trough in use with hold-downs in place

Boiling Trough

The boiling trough above was made of 24-gauge galvanized tin and soldered with soft solder. It was made by a tinsmith for ten dollars.

Lay out the pattern on the sheet of metal and cut to shape. Bend to the final shape and solder the end seams. Soft solder will work as long as there is water in the trough when it is heated. The handles shown are useful but not essential.

A pair of hold-downs can be fashioned from a waste piece of tin. Do not make them from any ferrous metal.

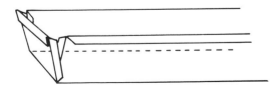

Fig. 25   Trough pattern

Fig. 26 *Lever down, pressure off*

Guitar-Maker's Clamps

Deep-throat clamps, an essential guitar-making tool, are easy to make. They fit through the sound hole for clamping the bridge and are also used to clamp fan bracing. Only one is absolutely necessary, but their convenience and simplicity justify the additional investment in time for building several. A similar clamp is available from H. L. Wild Co. (see page 94), but the price of one will pay for four home-made clamps.

The clamp has a fixed lower and a movable upper jaw. When the clamp is fastened about an object, raising the lever brings pressure to bear. Pressure is released by flipping the lever down.

A $^{13}/_{16}$" $\times$ 3¾" $\times$ 45" length of birch or maple will make four clamps and leave a piece for making a purfling cutter. You also need a ¼" $\times$ 1" aluminum strip (sold in 6' lengths at hardware stores; this aluminum stock is also used for the end clamps of the bending form). Two dozen 1" rivets with recessed ends that can be peened over, plus four ½" cotter pins, complete the list.

Lay out the pattern (Fig. 29) and saw off

the end with the levers drawn on it. Rip down the center of the long remaining piece. Cut off each set of jaws. Mark, on each jaw, the oblong mortise that will receive the aluminum shaft. Drill a series of ¼" holes in each mortise and chisel through, working from both ends. When the slots are cleared, smooth the inner walls with a 1" flat file.

Cut four 10" pieces off the aluminum strip and de-burr the ends. Try the metal shaft in the upper jaw; it should ride freely up and down. The slot in the lower jaw is left snug enough that the metal shaft has to be driven in with light hammer blows.

Drill the $^{1}/_{16}$" hole at the mouth of the long kerf. Jigsaw the kerf through to this hole and smooth the inner face of this kerf with a folded piece of sandpaper slid back and forth.

Draw the lines for the tenon at the front end of the upper jaw. Clamp the jaw in a vise and insert a wedge into the kerf (Fig. 30). The wedge will permit you to saw off both cheeks of the tenon without scarring the bottom face of the long kerf.

Trace the outline of the lever and jigsaw.

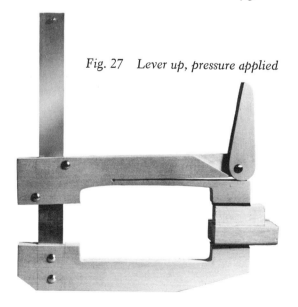

Fig. 27 *Lever up, pressure applied*

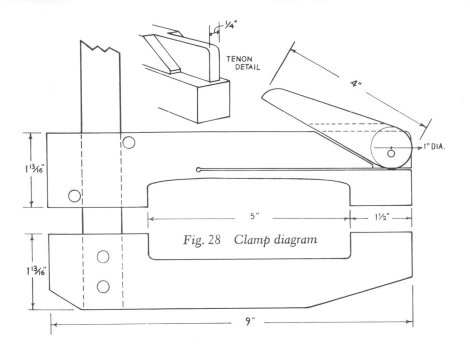

TENON DETAIL

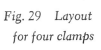

Fig. 28   Clamp diagram

Fig. 29   Layout
for four clamps

Sand the contours perfectly smooth and mark off the center mortise. Drill a ¼″ hole through the inner terminus of the mortise and then remove the mortise with two saw cuts down to the drill hole. Smooth the inner cheeks and make sure the lever moves freely around the tenon.

The operating principle of the clamp depends on pressure exerted on the flexible extension under the kerf. This pressure comes from the eccentric motion of the lever, which swings on an off-center axis.

Place the lever on the tenon in the down position and drill the off-center hole through lever and tenon. Insert a rivet and peen the end over.

Drive the aluminum shaft into the lower jaw, drill two holes, and rivet. Slip on the upper jaw and drill the two holes that fall on either side of the shaft. Fasten rivets. These two rivets are positioned to keep the upper jaw rigid when pressure is applied. A small hole and cotter pin at the upper end of the shaft complete the clamp. Rubber squares cut from an old inner tube may be used to line the jaw faces.

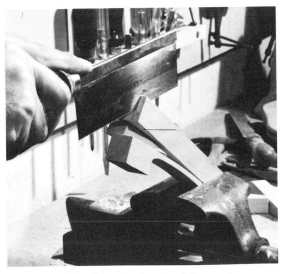

Fig. 30   Kerf wedged for sawing tenon

Purfling Cutter

A purfling cutter removes the corner segment around all four outer edges of the guitar. The depth and width of these cutout ledges depend on the kind of purfling design used. An adjustable purfling cutter designed for the violin trade is available (Fig. 11). It works well for guitars, but an equally effective cutter can be made from a piece of birch or maple and a saber-saw blade.

Slice a 1″ × 1¾₆″ × 4¾″ block open lengthwise and smooth both inner faces. Saw or chisel a groove down the center of side A. This groove must be wide enough to accommodate the saber-saw blade and shallow enough so that when the sides are bolted together sufficient pressure will be exerted to hold the blade firmly in place.

Saw the waste from around the pilot leg of side B and shape the pilot to the prescribed shape. Round the edges of all bearing surfaces to prevent gouging and marking.

Saber-saw blades can be sharpened to a fine cutting edge. The blade pictured is a Trojan S–32. Grind off the teeth along the edge for about ½″ above the cutting edge. In grinding the edge do not allow the blade to overheat and destroy the temper. Sharpen only one edge, the inner face.

Cut two horizontal grooves ⁵⁄₁₆″ wide on the back of side B. Cut two small strips of metal to act as long washers for the two bolts in each groove. With both sides clamped together, drill the four holes and bolt with ¾″ machine screws.

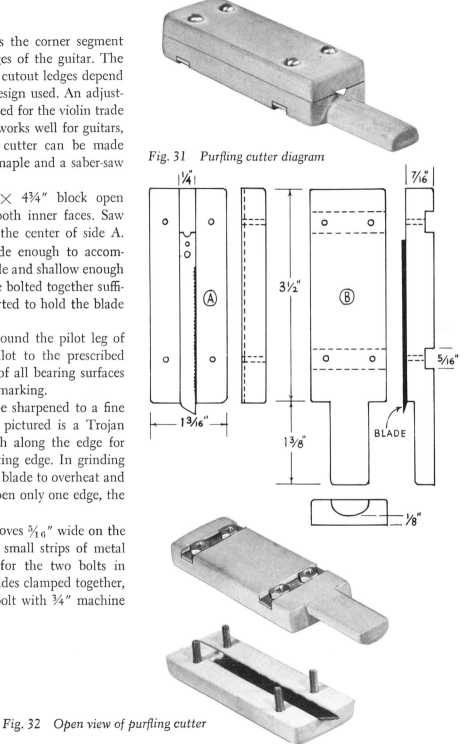

Fig. 31   Purfling cutter diagram

Fig. 32   Open view of purfling cutter

Glue

Animal or hide glue made from hoofs, bones, sinews, and skin linings of cattle has been the staple adhesive of instrument-makers for hundreds of years. This glue is manufactured in different grades of varying strength and comes in sheet, flake, chip, or granular form.

To prepare animal glue, place the glue in a double-jacket glue pot with enough cold water to cover and leave to soak. When the glue has absorbed as much water as it can hold, the glue pot is heated to a temperature which must not exceed 150°F. (Excessive heat destroys the strength of the glue. Repeated heating weakens and thickens the glue. Water must then be added, further weakening the glue.)

The best grades of hide glue prepared in this manner are strong and dependable. For optimum results the glue must be freshly made to the right consistency and temperature. Gluing must be done quickly in a warm room so that clamps can be applied before the glue jells.

Liquid hide glue is also available in ready-to-use form. It has many of the same qualities of hot glue without the elaborate preparations. Setting time is slower, permitting ample time for coating and assembly before clamping. The temperature of the workroom and wood should be above 60°F.

A number of plastic adhesives available today are also useful for instrument-making. They have different properties that make them valuable for certain purposes.

Plastic resin glue (Weldwood, Cascamite) is very strong, water-resistant, and easy to use. It comes in powder form and need only be mixed with water. When mixed, the glue has a usable life of five to seven hours at 70°F. For best results the glue, wood, and temperature should be at 70° or higher. At lower curing temperature full strength is not attained. Ade-

quate clamping pressure is necessary to insure intimate contacts of gluing surfaces. At 70°F. clamp hardwoods for five to seven hours, softwoods four to six hours. Higher curing temperatures will reduce the clamping time.

Polyvinyl resin glue (Elmer's Glue-All) is a white liquid glue that cures very quickly—twenty to thirty minutes at 70°F. It dries transparent and is quite strong. At temperatures below 60° the glue turns chalky white and the strength is affected. Polyvinyl glues are not as water resistant as plastic resin glues.

A *liquid resin glue* that has a very fast set and outstanding strength is a yellow glue sold as Titebond (Franklin Glue Co.). The author prefers this to white glues.

Transparent *epoxy cement* comes in two tubes, one a resin and the other a catalyst or hardener. The two are mixed in equal parts and applied in a thin coating to each gluing surface. Curing time is overnight and makes a permanent bond of unequaled strength.

Purists insist on the exclusive use of animal glue in the construction of stringed instruments, citing its organic nature and elasticity. Precisely this elasticity is what is responsible for the majority of instrument repairs—glue failure. Animal glue absorbs atmospheric moisture, and exposure to repeated cycles of dampness and drying ultimately weakens the glue. Scientific research has recently uncovered the fact that there are certain molds whose spores can live in animal glue. When present they eventually break down the glue.

Stradivarius used animal glue—the strongest glue then available—plus three and sometimes four nails to fasten the instrument's neck to the top block. There is no reason to suppose that he would not have welcomed the superior strength and durability of modern glues. Insistence on using only animal glue must inevitably be put down to a sentimental attachment for the old way.

Animal glues do have the advantage of making it easy to remove the plates (top and back) for repairs. A hot knife and some carefully applied moisture will separate a glued joint—although this is more meaningful for violins than guitars since a great many interior repairs can be made to a guitar through the sound hole.

Gluing is best accomplished by having both surfaces to be glued perfectly smooth. In laboratory tests conducted by the U.S. Department of Agriculture it was found that no benefit derived from intentional roughening of gluing surfaces.

Before gluing rosewood it is important to wash the surface with benzol (sold in stationery stores under the trade name Bestine) to remove as much surface wax and oil as possible. Moisten a clean rag with benzol and rub the rosewood until no more color comes off on the rag. A more effective glue joint will result.

Fig. 33   Eighteenth-century Venetian guitar (front and back)

Planing the Wood

Guitar sides and backs are sold in matched sets cut from the same log. They bear knife or saw marks and are at least $\frac{1}{8}$" thick. It is necessary to smooth both sides of the top and plane the sides and back to a full $\frac{5}{64}$".

The sides are scraped down first because they have to be bent.

Clamp the end of a side near the edge of the workbench. Remove the high spots with a plane adjusted to remove a small amount of wood at a time. Move the plane away from you, angled slightly to cut with a shearing action. Lift the plane, return to the beginning, and make another cut. If the plane bites badly into the wood, it is cutting against the grain; turn the board around and plane from the other end. Plane the surface until all rough saw and knife marks are gone.

When both sides are level, switch to the hand scraper. Draw the small hand scraper toward you, its blade angled for shear, and use both hands to guide and apply pressure (Fig. 34). Move the scraper in a systematic pattern that will insure an even removal of wood. Check the thickness as work proceeds. The large scraper blade is used for final smoothing and leveling. Sanding is not necessary.

Clamp both sides butted together and use the steel scraper blade over both. Turn them over and butt the other edges. Scrape them again to make both sides a uniform thickness. Beware of scraping the sides thinner than $\frac{5}{64}$". A thin spot in the sides can affect the tone. Flamenco-guitar sides are planed to a thickness of $\frac{1}{16}$" full.

Backs are not planed to thickness until they are jointed. Fasten the back to the work board used for the jointing operation. Drive tacks in along the perimeter—three or four will do—to hold the back while scraping.

Plane and scrape both sides, using the same procedure as on the sides. Because of the large area of the back it is necessary to check the level of the surface with a straightedge. Smooth the back to a thickness of a full $\frac{3}{32}$".

Smooth both sides of the jointed spruce top, removing only as much wood as necessary. At this stage the top must be left at its maximum smoothed thickness to accommodate the mosaic inlay easily. Smoothing also permits you to judge which side is best for use as the top face. Store tops and backs under a weighted board until they are strutted and braced. This will allow the wood to breathe but prevent warping. If an appreciable amount of time is going to elapse before resuming work (three or four weeks), shellac the end grain of top and back to retard moisture absorption.

Fig. 34   Scraping side with a hand scraper

Fig. 35   Planing back

Fig. 36   Final leveling with scraper blade

Jointing Top and Back

Guitar sound boards are joined along the edge on which the grain is narrowest. Close the two halves like a book and match the grain on the ends so that the halves are placed exactly as they were before being cut apart.

Clamp the boards in a vise and plane the edge to be joined as level as possible. Do not remove any more wood than necessary to accomplish this end.

A 2′ length of 1″ × 3″ lumber that is perfectly true in its long dimension will complete the jointing of the edges. Cut a sheet of #80-D (medium-grit) aluminum oxide paper into strips wide enough to glue along the 1″ edge of the 1″ × 3″ board. Paste the strips into place with white glue so that the edge of the board is one unbroken sanding surface. Fig. 37 shows an aluminum level being used. The sandpaper was glued to the edge with rubber cement.

Place one half of the sound board on top of the other, overlapping so that only one edge is brought into contact with the sandpaper. Hold down the two halves firmly with the left hand and slide the sanding edge back and forth against the edge of the sound board. Continue this motion until the edge looks true. Reverse the boards and sand the other edge. Butt the two edges together and hold the sound board up before a light. If light can be seen through the joint, repeat the sanding procedure until no light is visible through the joint.

With the boards butted, trace the outline of the template on each half. The best half of the sound board should fall in the lower bout. This area is the main vibrating surface and sound-producing portion of the sound board. Grain irregularities can sometimes be concealed under the fret board.

Lay the halves down on a ¾″ plywood board at least 20″ × 20″. Press the joint together and examine it closely. Sometimes the darker lines (summer growth) in the grain will meet in a disturbing pattern at the joint if the grain converges. Occasionally an unsightly heavy line will result from the bringing together of two dark lines. For the most unobtrusive joint sand the edges until they give the appearance of an unbroken grain pattern when butted.

Center the sound board on the plywood work

Fig. 37   Sanding edges with level faced with sandpaper

board. Drive five carpet tacks along the outer edge of one side so that their heads grip the board and hold it firm. If the edges are irregular, or not square enough to hold a tack well, plane them square. Put waxed paper under the joint and position a ¼″ × ¾″ batten centered under the joint. Position the other half of the sound board so the joint is closely butted over the batten. Drive in five tacks along the edge of this half, but not far enough to engage the wood and hold it. Remove this half of the sound board and apply a thin coating of clear epoxy cement to the edge of the joint. Remove the batten and coat the other half's edge with epoxy. Replace the batten, put the other half back into position, and hammer the tacks down until they grip the edge. Put a strip of waxed paper over the joint and pull out the batten. Clamp a board across the joint. For uniform pressure the clamping board should be slightly bowed. Beware of tightening the clamps so much the clamping board rises in the middle. Leave undisturbed overnight.

When removing the sound board do not proceed until the tacks have been removed from one edge. If the clamping board is removed without first lifting the tacks the top may fly up, leaving the annoying task of re-sanding the edges and gluing the halves together again.

Figs. 38 through 40 show a back being jointed. The basic procedure is identical with that described for the sound board. The only difference is the use of a center strip of inlay on the back, a traditional embellishment. A light strip is used with rosewood and a dark with maple or other light woods.

The veneer strip is trimmed to the thickness of the back. Epoxy cement is applied to both edges of the back and both sides of the veneer strip. The inlay and edges are clamped together.

Fig. 38   One edge tacked, batten in position

Fig. 39   Glue applied, both sides tacked

Fig. 40   Batten removed, joint under pressure

Fig. 41   Immersing sides

Bending Sides

There are two ways to bend guitar sides: wetting the wood and shaping it on a heated pipe or steeping the wood in boiling or nearly boiling water until plastic enough to clamp to a form.

Spanish luthiers have traditionally used an upright oval metal pipe heated by an enclosed charcoal brazier at the base. The chimney becomes hot and the moistened strips of wood are pressed against the hot metal and slowly worked into the pattern of the guitar. The success of this method depends on skill gained through practice. It is easy for a beginner to scorch or fracture the wood by undue pressure; the boiling method is much less hazardous. An additional advantage is the boiling away of some of the waxy content of rosewood, leaving the wood more amenable to glue. A boiling trough is required for either method.

Begin by aligning the two sides so that they are book-matched, forming a symmetrical design down the center. Place them on top of the bending form and rock them end-to-end to establish their centered position on the form. Make two or three short pencil marks across the center joint of the sides at the point where the incurved waist will fall. These marks will help position the wood on the form

quickly and prevent mismatching of the sides.

Pour two inches of water into the trough and set it on a stove so that it is heated by two burners. (A sheet of tin over the trough will speed heating of the water.) When the water is very hot (steam rising), immerse the two boards. Put in the hold-down brackets and cover the trough. An hour and a half of steeping will make the wood plastic enough to bend.

When the time is up, remove the boards (tongs and work gloves will make this operation painless) and position them on the bending form. The sides must lie on the form butted together and parallel to the sides of the form. Lay the canvas on top of the boards and position the waist block. Press the block down and engage the side bolts. Tighten these two bolts until the boards are within ¼″ of the form. Carefully pull the lower bout down, keeping the canvas taut and clamp the end (not too tight). Do the same to the upper bout. Now screw home the waist block and secure the end clamps.

Transfer of the hot, moist wood from trough to form should be done rapidly.

Place the form in a heated room or in the sun. The quicker the drying process the better. In periods of protracted humidity where drying is retarded, use heat lamps. If maple is allowed to remain wet for more than two or three days, mildew may form at the waist juncture, the last place to dry.

Leave the form undisturbed for a week. If the wood is properly dry it will come off the form with only moderate springback and fit into the mold. If the sides seem dry but go into the mold only with considerable difficulty, they will have to be placed in the squeeze jig.

Fig. 45 shows the squeeze jig in use. The waist curve has been padded with rubber to hold the sides in a curve more exaggerated than that of the bending form. The bouts are also bound and propped to an exaggerated degree, although following a natural curve. A few days in the squeeze jig will correct a difficult springback.

The success of the boiling method depends on the use of straight-grain, seasoned wood free of figure, planed to a uniform thickness. Highly flamed curly maple (because of its complex grain structure) will sometimes fracture at the waist if abrupt pressure is used. The fracture usually occurs on the inner face at the point of greatest compression. If it is only a surface break it can be filled and sanded smooth.

Wood that has been bent to a curve has a "memory." An increase in moisture content will tend to straighten a curve, a decrease will cause a curve to become sharper. Because of this, the almost flat section of the side that begins at the bottom of the waist curve and leads into the lower bout is the weakest part. This section is under stress from the sharp waist curve and the large curve of the lower bout. It is strongest at the edges where the linings hold it in shape. The weakest portion is the center, which sometimes becomes slightly concave.

Any deviation from the flat will be advertised by the distorted highlight on the final polished surface. The way to avoid this is by keeping the wood to be bent a full $\frac{5}{64}$" and leaving it on the form until dry and ready to use. (This problem may be related to the structural density of wood. The harder, denser varieties of Brazilian rosewood seem to have the most stable shape-retaining properties.)

Cleanse the trough soon after using or the gummy residue will dry and require scouring with steel wool to remove. The boiled-off residue of rosewood will also stain light wood if left in the trough.

Fig. 42   Lining up sides, waist block in place

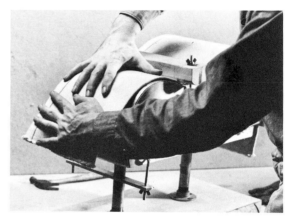

Fig. 43   Bending bout to form

Fig. 44   Tightening wing nut with wrench

Fig. 45   Sides propped and bound in squeeze jig

Fig. 46   Clamping tail block

Fig. 47   Bottom inlay in place

Side Assembly

After the sides are bent they are clamped in the mold. Mark the center of the overlap top and bottom, and saw off the excess. The sides should now fit in the mold butted top and bottom. With both joints on the center line, inspect the contour. The fit should be snug or nearly so.

Make a tail block from the 1″ × 3″ × 4″ block of basswood, the grain running the long way. Shape the round front of the tail block with rasp and sanding stick. Round the back slightly. Hold or tape a piece of medium-grit sandpaper against the curved back where the block will glue. Grip the block in an upright position and rub it against the sandpaper until it conforms to the curve of the back.

Jigsaw the two clamping cauls that will facilitate clamping the tail block during gluing (Fig. 46). Slip a piece of waxed paper between mold and sides to keep them from gluing together. Apply plastic resin glue to both surfaces and clamp.

A decorative strip of inlay is customarily applied to the bottom joint. It conceals the center joint and works into the purfling on top and bottom.

Glue up a ³⁄₁₆″ × 4″ strip of rosewood with a strip of white-black purfling along each long edge. Do this on waxed paper using push pins to hold the white-black strips against the rosewood.

Transfer the width of the inlay to the bottom joint. Clamp the sides in a vise with the joint facing up. Hold a try square against each mark and saw to the depth of the inlay. Chisel and level the groove with the edge of a file. If the saw cuts are a trifle scant the inlay should go in with some slight pressure. Glue with white glue.

The sides are now ready to be joined to the neck.

Neck

The unique design of the classic guitar neck gives it great strength and stability through the use of a foot that extends into the body of the guitar for about 3″. The bottom of this foot glues to the back and damps lateral and vertical movement of the neck. It also lends rigidity close to the point where the full force of sound waves coming through the sound hole strike the back.

The laminated construction of the foot is also much stronger than a one-piece neck would be. At concert pitch the neck is under a tensile strain of about 120 pounds, so strength is important.

Commercially produced guitars employ a block—often enormous—glued inside the guitar with a mortised slot to receive the dovetailed end of the neck. If the joint is loose, wooden shims are inserted to keep the neck in alignment during gluing. This method of joining, borrowed from violin construction, works well with the violin's proportionately shorter neck made of dense hardwood and subjected to much less string tension. The classic guitar neck, while more difficult to make, is unquestionably better adapted to the special requirements of the guitar.

The neck and head are joined and shaped as a unit before being joined to the foot section. The head profile, slots, and tuning machine holes are completed before the foot is glued on.

The neck is made from a 3″ × 42″ piece of straight-grain Honduras mahogany dressed to ⅞″. This is slightly thicker than the standard $1\frac{3}{16}$″ but is necessary to laminate the foot to the proper thickness of 3½″. If only the standard thickness is available, a 3″ × 48″ piece dressed to $1\frac{1}{16}$″ full may be used. This will add one more layer to the lamination, which is perfectly acceptable.

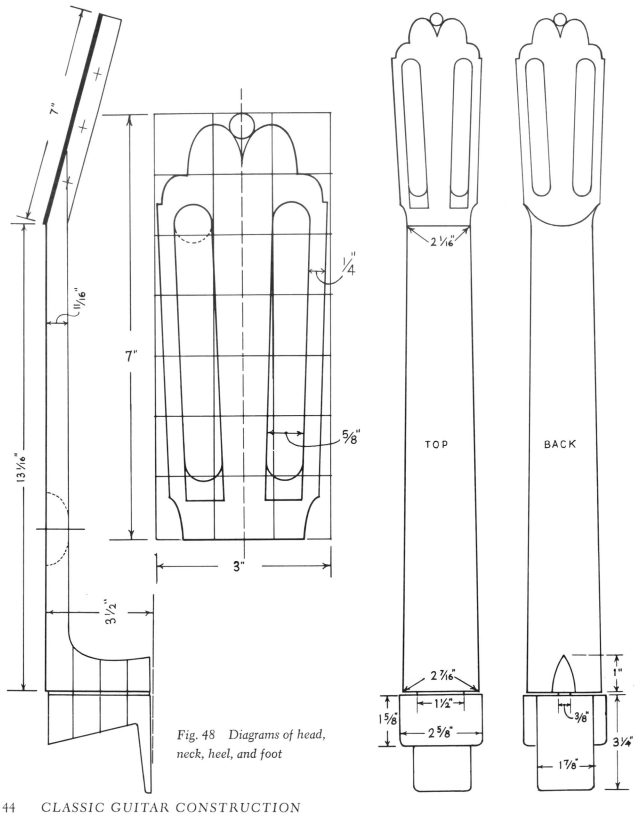

Fig. 48 *Diagrams of head,
neck, heel, and foot*

Cut off a 25″ length of mahogany and 7½″ from one end mark off a 2½″ segment:

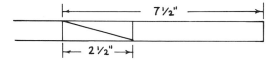

Continue the lines down both sides of the board as a guide for sawing. Stand the board on edge and clamp. Saw down through the board on the angle formed by the line bisecting the 2½″ rectangle (Fig. 49). Reverse the smaller piece and place it on top of the longer piece so that the oblique cut makes a continuous line:

Clamp the two pieces on the edge of a workbench and plane their angled face smooth and square. Check with try square to make sure the sawed edges along the 3″ dimension are all true. Reverse their positions:

Glue the head to the neck, using the set-up in Fig. 50. Apply plastic resin glue to each face and clamp vertically on each end. Keep the vertical clamps loose until the glued faces of the joint are in contact. Tighten the vertical clamps and apply the horizontal clamps, using cauls. The vertical clamps are used to resist the outward pressure of the horizontal clamps on the angled joint. A piece of waxed paper under the joint will prevent gluing to the workbench.

When dry, clamp again to the edge of a workbench so that the inclined end protrudes out from the bench. Plane and sand the face of the head to a thickness of ½″.

The head of the guitar is where luthiers have traditionally applied their hallmark; the profile of the head identifies the maker. It is a point of pride, and a well-balanced design requires thoughtful consideration.

The design used here is the result of many sketches and earlier abandoned designs. It has a pleasing symmetry that echoes classical Spanish motifs. The small ball on top may be omitted without harm to the basic design.

Glue a 3¼″ × 7½″ piece of ¹⁄₁₆ rosewood and holly veneer together. When dry, glue this sandwich to the face of the head, leaving a

Fig. 49   Cutting off head piece

Fig. 50   Clamping head piece to neck

Fig. 51   Clamping face veneers

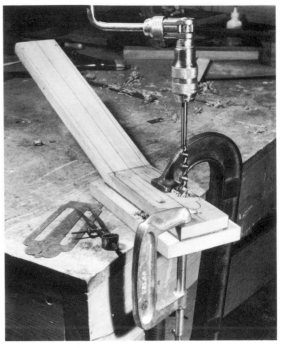

Fig. 52   Drilling holes at both ends of slots

minimum of ⅛″ overhang over the top face of the neck. This overhang will later be sawed off at a right angle to the face of the neck to serve as a backstop for the nut.

The glued-up head is then held in a vise while the excess veneer is trimmed from the sides with a plane. Draw a pencil line down the center of the head and neck on both back and front. Transfer the head pattern to the back of the head. In doing so, take careful account of any discrepancy in length between the back and front of the head. With a try square run a pencil line from the top of the design, across the back, up the sides, and onto the top face. Lay the pattern against this line and make sure the design is accurately placed. Position the centers of the four ⅝″ holes on the back and scribe the circles with a compass. Draw the lines for the long slots, making sure they do not fall closer to the edge than ¼″. Clamp the head face down to a board to prevent fracturing of the face veneer and drill the four ⅝″ holes.

Saw off the face veneer overhang perpendicular to the top face of the neck. Use a fine back saw with a try square as a saw guide.

Saw off the tapered excess at the sides and

jigsaw the outline of the head. Smooth the sides of the head and mark the positions of the holes for the tuning-machine shafts.

The standard spacing for tuning-machine shafts is 1½″ on centers. The machine in Fig. 53 has a spacing of 1⁷⁄₁₆″ on centers. Check the spacing of your set before drilling holes. Measure from the center of the shaft-screw set in each gear. (The standard diameter of shafts is ⅜″, they require ¹³⁄₃₂″ holes. Here again it is wise to ascertain the shaft diameter of your set before drilling holes.)

A drill press is best for drilling these six holes. They must be drilled at right angles to the tapered sides; if drilled slightly askew, the machines will not turn easily.

With a jig or coping saw remove the long pieces of waste wood between the ⅝″ holes.

Fig. 53 Construction sequence of head

Fig. 54 Gluing neck to foot section

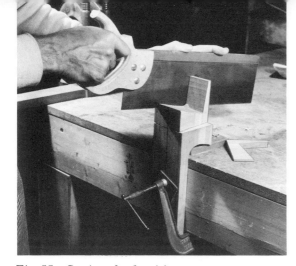

Fig. 55 *Sawing cheeks of foot*

Fig. 56 *Sawing out front section*

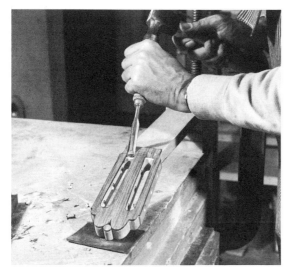

Fig. 57 *Chiseling ramp at base of slot*

Clamp the head in a vise and smooth the inner faces of these channels with a sanding stick. Try the tuning machines in place to make sure they operate smoothly. If a peg is hard to turn, it may be that the shaft is out of alignment or the holes are not true. Now is the time to make minor adjustments to insure proper functioning of the tuning machines.

Glue this neck member to the four- (or five-) piece lamination that comprises the foot. Apply plastic resin glue to all gluing surfaces and clamp. Figure 54 illustrates the method of clamping using lateral clamps and cauls over waxed paper to prevent horizontal shifting while applying the vertical clamps.

When glued, plane the sides of the foot square with the neck and draw all guide lines with soft pencil on the neck: the exact taper of the neck, the position of the juncture with the body, the shape of the heel and the vertical cut on each side of the foot marking the point of entry of the guitar sides.

Use a large back saw to make the vertical cuts that will accommodate the sides. This cut is made at a slight angle because the sides are curved at this juncture. Saw carefully and slowly, checking progress of the blade as it approaches the marks denoting the terminal points at both ends of the slot.

Saw away the large waste areas around the heel. The arch of the heel is best removed by band saw but can be cut away with the large gouge.

Shape the heel to approximately its final form, using the gouges and rasp. Keep it symmetrical and work to within a full 1/16" of the pencil line on the neck that marks where the fret board will lie.

A simple template will guarantee symmetry of the heel curve. Cut some cardboard to the contour of the curve and use it as a guide.

Cut away the largest chunks of waste wood with the 1" gouge struck by hammer or mallet

(Fig. 59). As the shape becomes more clearly defined, switch to the ½″ gouge. Properly sharpened it will cut easily with hand pressure alone. Place both feet squarely and use the weight and leverage of the entire torso to work the tool. Dig the gouge in with a rocking motion so that it will bite and exit in short cuts. Do not try to take out too much in one cut. Guide the blade with a firm grip of the left hand and apply pressure with the handle held securely under the heel of the right palm.

As the long curve that will butt against the sides takes shape, beware of dislodging large splinters with the chisel—this is easy to do when the edge of the gouge is cutting parallel to the grain. Switch to a folded piece of sandpaper for final shaping of this curve.

Trim away excess wood along the length of the neck to within a full ¹⁄₁₆″ of the fret-board guidelines.

Clamp the completed neck to the workbench and chisel away the exit ramps at the base of the tuning-machine slots (Fig. 57). Make cuts to the proper depth on both sides of each slot with the fine back saw. Chisel the ramps with a ½″ chisel struck by a mallet. A pad of rubber or a folded cloth under the head will prevent damage.

Finish the exits with a flat file. The brown and white veneer lines should make a straight line parallel to the sawed-off edge that backstops the nut.

A simpler exit can be made by using a round file to file a rounded chute instead of the squared-off ramp. It is just as satisfying a solution and is used by many luthiers. It was used by the gifted luthier Marcelo Barbero in the head shown in Fig. 58.

The neck is complete for the moment. The head may be carefully smoothed and finished but the underside of the neck is left untouched, the surface left flat for efficient clamping of the fret board.

Fig. 58   Head by Marcelo Barbero

Fig. 59   Rough shaping with gouge

Joining Sides to Neck

Transfer dimensions of the distances between the top and bottom termini of the slots to the top and bottom of the sides (Fig. 60). Saw off the tapered segment that falls equally on each side of the top juncture of the sides. Sand the ends of the sides to a gradual taper until they fit securely in their slots. The slot itself can be enlarged by using a file made of sandpaper glued to each side of a flat piece of sheet metal. Sanding the sides of the slot must be done in a way that will not round or disfigure the slot entrance. If this occurs there will be a gap between heel and sides.

Fit the sides in place and place the entire assembly in the mold. Clamp the neck to the mold centered on the longitudinal mold axis. If the sides are difficult to get into the mold, cut some more wood from the ends of the sides. It is not absolutely essential that the sides fit snugly around the entire inner contour of the mold. You must, however, maintain

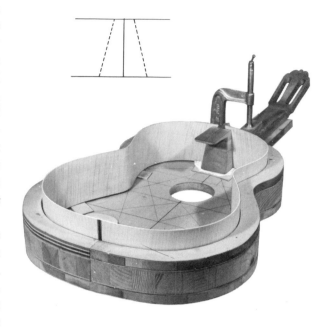

Fig. 60   Neck and sides being glued together

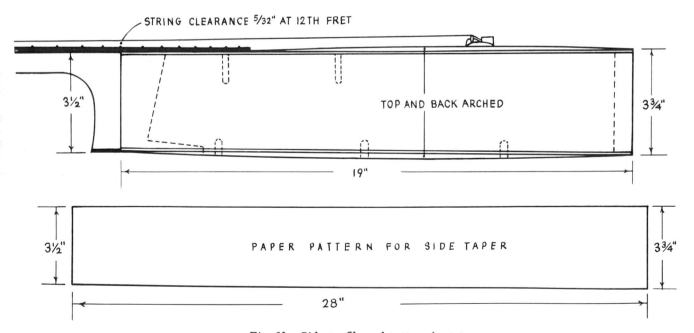

STRING CLEARANCE 5/32" AT 12TH FRET

3½"

TOP AND BACK ARCHED

3¾"

19"

3½"

PAPER PATTERN FOR SIDE TAPER

3¾"

28"

Fig. 61   Side profile and pattern for taper

symmetry. If there is a gap on one side and none on the other, some additional cutting of the end of the side that is tight against the mold is required.

Apply hide glue to the inner surfaces of the slot and the ends of the sides. Fit the sides in place and return the assembly to the mold with the neck clamped on dead center. A caul and waxed paper are inserted under the recessed table to keep the sides from protruding. Additional cauls are placed under the sides at strategic points to equalize this discrepancy and keep the sides level. With try square resting on the floor of the mold, make certain that the sides rise vertically. Allow sides to dry.

To find the taper of the bottom edge of the sides draw a pattern of a flat side on a piece of heavy paper (Fig. 61). Cut out this pattern and position it on one side, its bottom edge lined up with the joint behind the tail block. Affix the pattern to the side with masking tape, keeping the horizontal edge of the pattern aligned with the top edge. Cut off the excess

where the paper meets the neck. Run a pencil or white crayon along the bottom edge of the pattern denoting the taper of the side. Reverse the pattern and follow the same procedure on the other side.

Return the neck-side assemby to the mold and clamp the neck. Replace the cauls that prop up the sides. Plane off the excess wood down to the taper line on both sides. Then rest the work board on top of the sides to accomplish final leveling of the sides. Use the flat work board continually to check for gaps between the sides and the bottom of the work board. Use a sanding stick for final leveling (Fig. 62).

For the moment, the tail block, foot, and heel are tapered in the same plane as the sides. Later the sides will have to be pared down below the level of the foot to accommodate the arch of the back.

When the entire contour fits flush against the bottom of the work board the sides are ready to receive the lining.

Fig. 62   Leveling top of sides with sanding stick

Linings

Linings provide a broader gluing surface and strengthen the curved sides. The lining that joins top to sides is a continuous strip kerfed (partly sawed through) at intervals of ¼". The lining that joins back to sides is a smooth unbroken band.

Corners are the least efficient areas in an acoustic chamber; it is important to neutralize them to avoid undesirable resonances. An unbroken lining between back and sides gives rigidity and strength where they are needed; the back and sides must be as stable as possible. Basswood, a fibrous, cottony wood, is ideal for lining because it is acoustically dead and can be bent more easily than mahogany.

Factory-made guitars employ a kerfed lining top and bottom because of the ease with which they can be installed. The notion that a kerfed lining permits freer vibration of the top is dubious. From the standpoint of acoustics, an unbroken lining top and bottom is probably the best arrangement—it was often used by the great German guitar-maker Hermann Hauser.

Lining is obtainable cut to the proper triangular shape or it can be ripped from a 30" length of ⅝" basswood. The kerfs can be cut

Fig. 63   Kerfing on machine

by power saw or by hand using a back saw. In Fig. 63 a strip of white tape serves as a guide for spacing the cuts. Each cut is positioned over the edge of the tape to bring the next cut into position under the saw.

Lining is always installed with the sides in the mold.

Fit the kerfed lining in place with spring clothespins. Start at the waist and apply clothespins every few inches until the tail block and neck are reached. The tail-block end of the lining is let into the tail block, an operation designed to foreclose the possibility of the lining working loose at this inaccessible point in the guitar.

Chisel a ⅛"-deep mortise in the tail block shaped like the lining. Cut off the lining and fit it into the mortise. Now cut and fit the neck end of the lining which is not mortised. Butt this end neatly against the neck. This requires careful shaping of the lining to a compound angle. When this is done, examine the lining along its entire length to make sure that it fits well.

Fit the lining to the opposite side in the same manner.

The linings are glued in place with plastic resin glue. Do not permit the linings to drop below the top edge. If the kerfed lining breaks, as it often does, keep it tight and glue the fracture when applying glue to the lining. Clean off excess glue with a damp cloth. Check the under side of the lining with a flexible mirror and wipe away excess glue. If clothespins are used, apply helper clamps to squeeze out gaps.

A simple clamping jig will permit the use of small C clamps instead of clothespins. The most indifferent clamp is immeasurably more effective than a clothespin. This jig (Fig. 69) is used with a continuous outside caul stripped from a discarded rosewood side.

The bottom lining is made from flat strips

Fig. 64   Neck-side assembly with lining

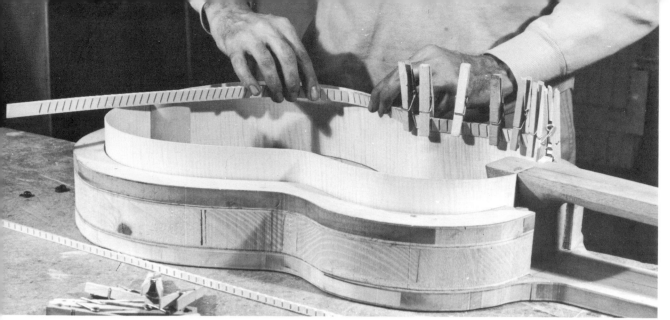

Fig. 65   Fitting kerfed top lining

of basswood ⁵⁄₃₂" × ⁵⁄₈" × 30". They are plasticized by the boiling method and bent on the bending form. Boil the wood for two hours.

In the process of bending the lining occasionally fractures at the waist. If the break is a superficial surface fracture, the lining need not be discarded. Apply glue to the break and clamp when gluing in the lining.

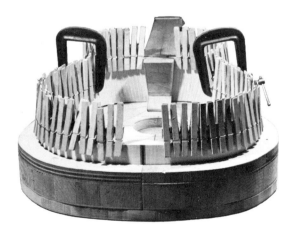

Fig. 66   Clamping with spring clothespins and helper clamps

Fit the bottom lining, using the procedure followed for the top lining. The tail block is again mortised and the upper end of the lining butts against the foot. Fig. 67 shows the bottom lining being glued with a series of small C clamps. The continuous outside caul is used to keep the sides from being scarred. Clamp indentations on the face of the lining itself are not serious because they will be removed when the lining is shaped. Spring clothespins may be used for clamping the bottom lining, but unless the bent lining conforms precisely to the contour of the side, clothespins alone will not do a good job. Use C clamps and cauls to pull the lining tight against the side wherever it bulges.

When dry, carve the bottom lining to a rounded shape (Fig. 68). Rough out the shape with a sharp knife and finish with sandpaper. Do not remove any wood from the bottom edge of the lining. This will decrease the gluing surface that will hold the back.

Fill all gaps in the lining with a mixture of fine sawdust and plastic resin glue. Scrape away all glue that may have dripped onto the inner surface of the sides and sand them smooth.

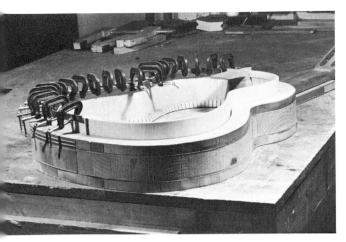

Fig. 67 *Clamping bottom lining*

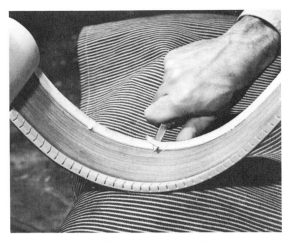

Fig. 68 *Carving bottom lining to shape*

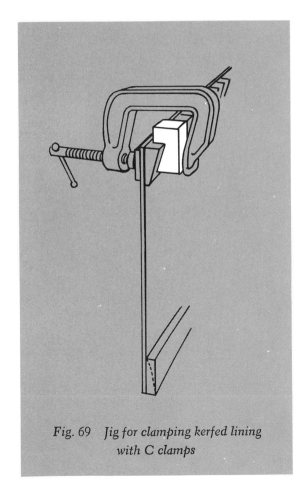

Fig. 69 *Jig for clamping kerfed lining with C clamps*

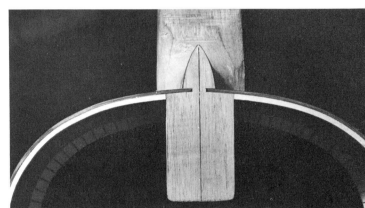

Fig. 70 *Lining at bottom of foot*

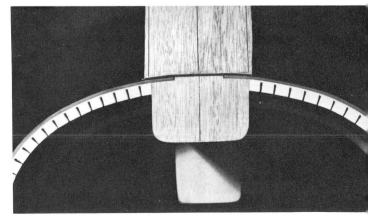

Fig. 71 *Lining at top of foot*

Sound-Board Construction

Place the neck-side assembly face down on the jointed top in perfect alignment with the center line. Clamp the neck and the tail block to keep the sides from shifting. Trace the inner and outer contours of the sides, showing the position of the foot and linings.

Remove the neck-side assembly and jigsaw the sound board along the outside pencil line. Turn the board over and locate the center of the 3⅜" sound hole. Scribe a circle with a 1¹¹⁄₁₆" radius. Measure the inner and outer diameter of your rosette. Scribe these circles on the sound board with a pencil compass. In scribing the circles for the groove that will receive the rosette it is best to work scant. If your rosette turns out to be too large to fit in the groove, the groove can be enlarged—it cannot be made smaller. The groove should fit snug enough to require gentle forcing to get the rosette in.

Fig. 72   *Removing sound hole with circle cutter*

Cut the rosette circles to a depth of ⅟₂₈" (standard veneer thickness). Cut the sound-hole circle to the same depth. The sound hole is not cut through until the rosette is inlaid. The rest of the waste wood in the groove is removed with a router bit. For drill-press operations the sound board should be secured to a work board with tacks at strategic points along the perimeter.

A circle cutter can be worked with a hand brace to cut the inner and outer edges of the groove. The waste wood can then be removed with a sharp ½" chisel. It is an exacting operation but can be done with surprising accuracy if the operator proceeds slowly with care.

As a rule, a small segment will have to be cut from the rosette to make it go into the groove. Make this cut at the least attractive point in the rosette. Try the fit of the rosette before gluing it in. Position the rosette so that the cut portion and other flaws fall in the area that will be concealed by the fret board.

Coat the groove with white glue and press the rosette into place. Tap the rosette home with a mallet over a wooden caul to receive the blows. Quickly, while the glue is still wet, raise some fine spruce sawdust by sanding near the rosette. Press this sawdust into any gaps along the edge of the rosette. Place waxed paper over the rosette and a weighted board to apply pressure.

When dry (45 minutes), level the rosette with the top of the sound board. Sand it down almost level with the surface of the top. Complete the leveling process with a single-edge razor blade used as a scraper. Sandpaper will wear away the softer spruce much faster than the hardwood mosaic and will also grind darker woods of the mosaic into the lighter woods. The razor blade will produce a clean, smooth finish.

The back of the sound board must now be planed down until the board is ³⁄₃₂" thick.

Fig. 73   *Braced underside of sound board*

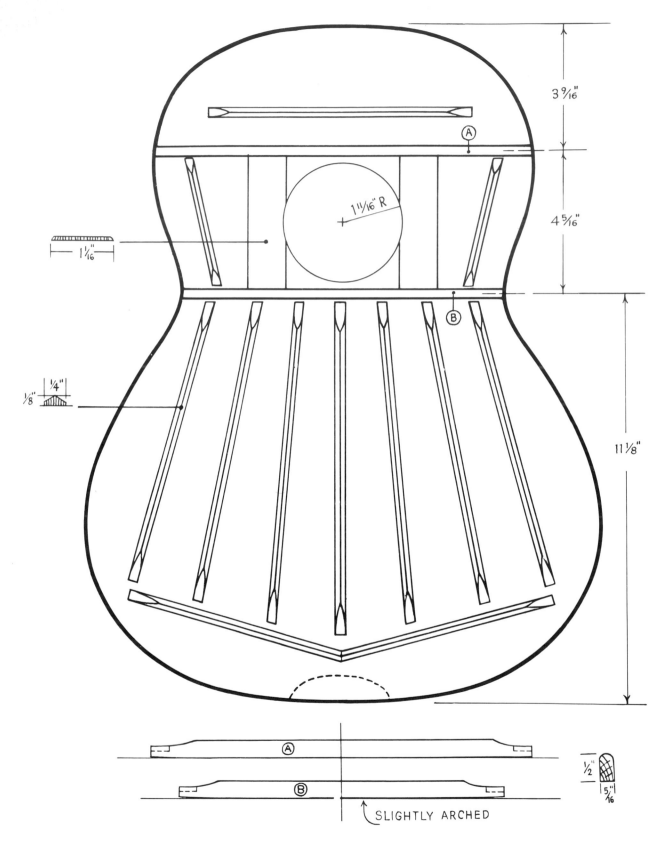

3 9/16"

1 11/16" R

4 5/16"

1 1/16"

1/4"

1/8"

11 1/8"

Ⓐ

Ⓑ

Ⓐ

Ⓑ

SLIGHTLY ARCHED

1/2"

5/16"

Fig. 74   Diagram of strutting and bracing for top

Fig. 75   *Sound board ready to receive rosette*

Fasten the sound board to a work board with the usual tacking method, being careful not to let the tackheads bite the edge. Scrape with hand scrapers, steel scraper blade, and finally with sandpaper. Check constantly to assure a level surface. Examine the edges to see that they are of a uniform thickness. Cut out the sound hole.

Carefully delineate the positions of the cross struts and the fan bracing. A triangle or rafter square held against the center line will give right-angle lines for the cross struts. Use a soft pencil for all markings. Clamp the work board to the workbench. Clamp the top to the work board with the holes aligned.

The fan bracing is glued into position first.

Cut all the braces to size and sand their gluing side smooth. Cut a ¼" × ½" × 7" piece of wood to use as a clamping caul to exert even pressure over the length of each brace. Sand the under side of this caul slightly concave so that when a clamp is applied over its middle it will exert pressure out to the ends (Fig. 77).

Apply a liberal coat of Titebond or white glue to a brace and press it into place with hand pressure. Hold it in place for about 20 seconds. Position the gluing caul and apply pressure with the deep-throat clamp. For added insurance apply a clamp at each end. A loose brace can cause buzzing in a guitar. Glue each brace in this manner, carefully scraping away all squeezed-out glue before it dries. Clamping time for braces is 30 minutes.

Place a narrow protective strip of metal or plastic alongside the first brace and chisel the brace to its pyramid shape. If the chisel bites, switch to the opposite direction. Use the angled

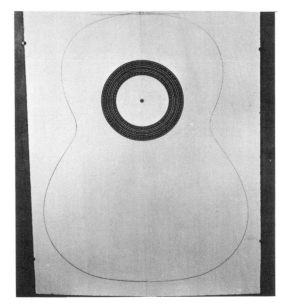

Fig. 76   Ready for jigsawing to shape

chisel and finish with fine sandpaper. Scoop out the ends of each brace with the angled chisel or the ½″ gouge. Leave a thin edge at each end.

Fashion the flat wide braces that glue on either side of the sound hole. Glue them in place with clamps working through the center hole. Chisel the long edges to a bevel and round off with sandpaper.

Glue the two cross struts in place, using the arrangement in Fig. 79. A ½″ × ½″ × 14″ clamping caul is used under the sound board when gluing the struts in. A slightly concave clamping caul is again employed for even pressure. Make sure the bottom arched surface of each strut is square and fits snugly before gluing. Chisel out the scooped ends after gluing. Each strut should have an end overhang of ¼″. Bevel the edges of the struts with the 3½″ block plane and sandpaper.

Go over all the bracing with fine sandpaper. Make sure all parts are glued tight.

The top is now complete and henceforth must be treated with care. Avoid excessive handling and sweep clean every surface on which it is laid. All the woods used in guitar construction are harder than the spruce top. If it is carelessly set down on an unnoticed speck of rosewood the face will be dented.

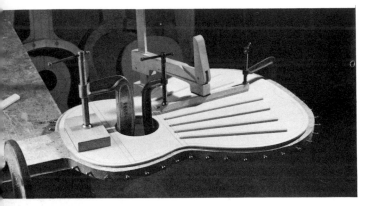

Fig. 77   Clamping braces

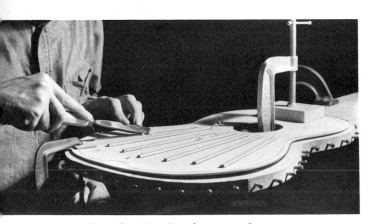

Fig. 78   Chiseling braces to shape

Fig. 79   Clamping cross struts

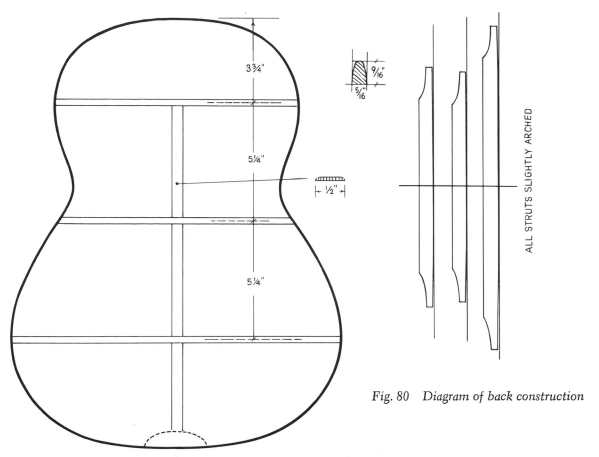

Fig. 80   *Diagram of back construction*

Back Construction

Jigsaw the back to shape and sand both sides satin-smooth. Strips of cross-grain wood are pieced together and glued over the center line of the back. When glued their edges are beveled and sanded smooth. Chisel out the places where the cross struts intersect the center strip. Glue the struts down, using the same procedure used for the top. The top of the center strip butts against the top cross strut.

When gluing struts beware of their shifting out of line when clamping pressure is applied. Back struts overhang ¼", as does the top.

This is the time to write in your name and the date.

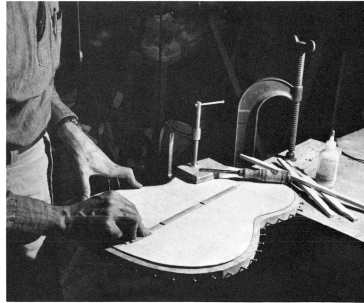

Fig. 81   *Sanding center strip*

Gluing Top and Back

Clamp the neck-side assembly to the work board, top side up. Lay the sound board in position aligned on center line. Hold the top in place and run a pencil line on each side of the cross struts where they intersect the sides. Also mark the point where the strut ends rest on the joint between linings and sides.

Saw off the excess, observing the curve where the struts will fit against the sides. Saw out the perpendicular cuts in the lining to free the small segment where each strut will fit. Chisel out these sections and carefully drop the top into position.

The commonest error in fitting top to sides is to force the sides apart. With the top in place, check the vertical rise of the sides to make sure they have not been splayed. The top end of the sound board has to be fitted against the back of the recessed table at the foot of the neck. Now check the other common source of difficulty in fitting the top—the tail block. If the top of the tail block lies lower than the top edge of the sides, it will not glue to the top. If the tail block is too high (more often the case) it will make an unsightly hump. Sight along the edges with the top held in place to locate discrepancies. Sand the top of the tail block until it is just right. Hold the guitar with a hand gripping each end and turn it over. See that the top butts smoothly against the tail block and the lining. Also make sure that the top lies snug against the foot of the neck.

With enough support under the neck to keep it level with the top, clamp the neck-side assembly to the work board preparatory to gluing. Position the top and secure it with a rubber band on each side of the neck stretched down to the bottom of the guitar, as well as one across the waist. Make a final examination of the fit to ascertain that the top will glue to the sides without any gaps.

Apply hide or plastic resin glue to the top edge of the lining, the tail block, foot, and inside edges of the openings in the lining where the strut ends butt. Use a small flat brush to apply glue quickly. Lay it on with a gentle, patting motion to keep glue from leaking down the saw kerfs. Apply glue to the areas in the top that show the outlined position of linings, foot, and tail block.

Press the top into place and secure with two lengthwise rubber bands and one across the waist. Check the plane of the neck with a straightedge. It must be level with the top down to the beginning of the sound hole. With the flat side of the straightedge make sure the center line on the neck is aligned with the center joint of the sound board down to the foot of the guitar. When precisely positioned, clamp the neck and complete the binding up of the top with rubber bands (Fig. 84).

Cut four brackets of Sitka spruce to support and reinforce the cross struts where they rest against the sides (Fig. 85). Cut each bracket so that the foot that fits into the end mortise of each strut is ¼″ oversize. The upright portion of each bracket must be filed and sanded to the curve of the side to which it will glue before fitting the foot to the mortise. Use the sandpaper-against-the-side technique to sand the back of the uprights to the exact curve.

When the back of the bracket fits perfectly, cut the foot to a slide fit in the mortise. Shape the bracket to its final shape before gluing it in place. It is extremely awkward to shape the bracket after it has been glued. If the brackets fit tight, clamping is unnecessary. Coat all gluing surfaces with a thin layer of epoxy and glue the brackets in place.

An upright reinforcing brace is sometimes glued to the side of the lower bout five or six inches back from the tail block. The real value of this procedure is questionable except in con-

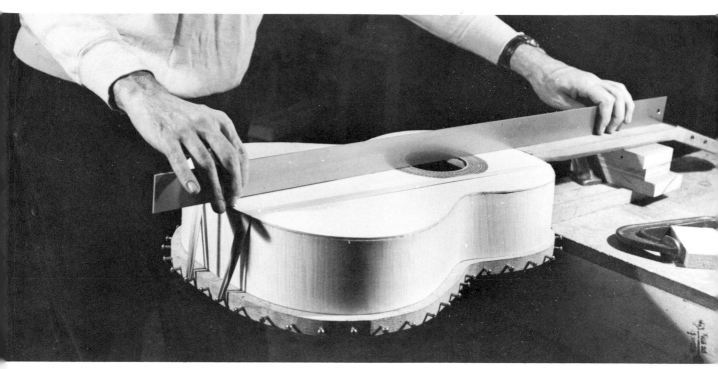

Fig. 82   *Checking plane of neck and top*

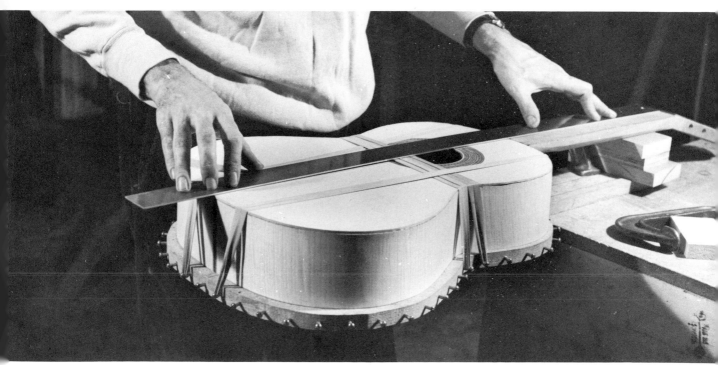

Fig. 83   *Centering neck*

Fig. 84 Clamping glued top

ends rest on the glue joint between lining and side. Cut off the strut ends so they fit the curve of the side they will butt. Mark off the depth and width of each strut end on the lining. Cut these mortises to receive the strut ends. The fit of these ends may be observed through the sound hole by illuminating the interior with a light held over the sound board.

With the back in place, loop rubber bands about the sound chest to hold the back secure. Look through the sound hole with a flexible mirror and gauge the gap between foot and back. This gap represents the amount of taper that has to be removed at the heel end of the foot. Remove the back and sand the foot to a gradual taper down to the heel. Use the sanding stick and taper the sides out to the middle of the upper bouts to a corresponding degree. Guard against lowering one side more than the other. As sanding progresses, replace the back to check the fit. The ends of the struts will have to be filed down to fit into the mortises made shallower by the lowered sides. This procedure must be repeated until the back lies snug against the foot, the linings, and the tail

structing flamenco guitars, with their more fragile construction. Torres used an upright side brace in the almost-flat sections on each side of the waist curve—an attempt, evidently, to defeat the "memory" stress referred to on page 41. He also bracketed each back cross strut, an operation that requires gluing on top and back simultaneously.

Side reinforcing braces are made of spruce or basswood, $5/16''$ $\times$ $1/8''$ and the height of the space between linings. They must be rounded to fit the contour and glued. After gluing, the top and bottom ends of the brace are beveled to meet the lining.

The back is fitted in much the same manner as the top. Additional difficulty in fitting the back stems from the need to fair the foot, sides, and tail block to accommodate the arch of the back. The foot and the sides close to the foot have to be tapered down toward the heel to glue properly to the back.

Position the back and mark where the strut

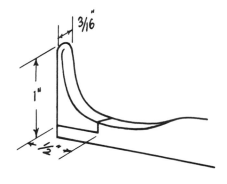

Fig. 85 Cross strut bracket

Fig. 86   Interior view of guitar with brackets

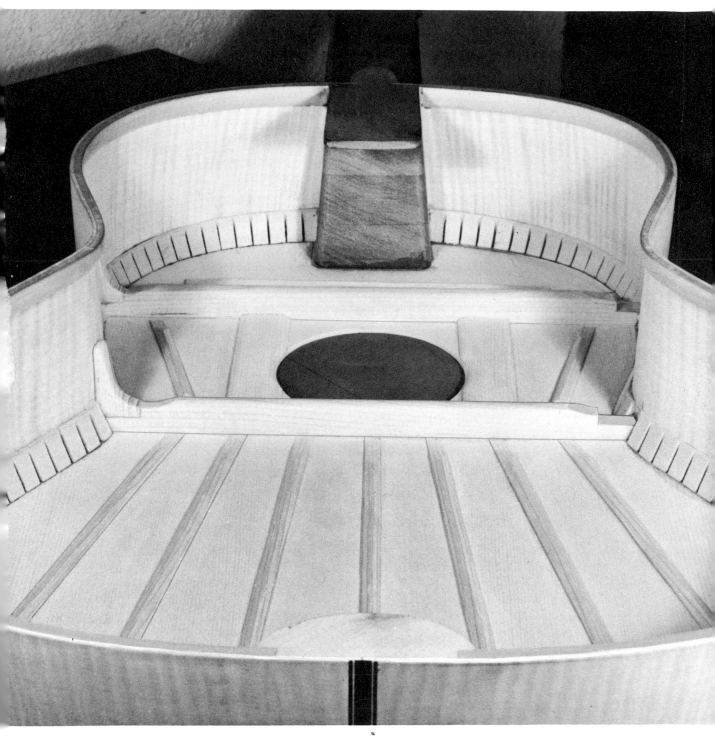

block and the strut ends are seated in their mortises.

Fitting the arched back is the most exacting and tedious part of guitar assembly. Work slowly with deliberate care. The most common hazard is the careless removal of too much wood from either upper bout, necessitating a compensatory planing of the sides down to the tail block.

Guitars are often made with flat backs, thus simplifying the fitting operation, but they do not sound as good as guitars with arched backs. A rounded acoustic chamber is better than a square one. Arching also helps stabilize the back by placing it under slight stress.

Before gluing the back in place, go over the entire interior of the guitar with fine sandpaper. Scrape away glue drippings and smooth all rough surfaces. Roughness attracts dust and dust attracts moisture.

It is advisable to use hide glue in gluing the back even though plastic resin glue was used for the top. This will make it easy to open the guitar if the need should arise, the back being much easier to remove than the top.

Alternate Assembly Method

Assemble sides and tail block in the regular way. Fit the sides to the neck but do not glue. Jigsaw the completed sound board to the exact inner contour of the mold and drop it into the mold face down. With the sides fitted into the neck, drop the whole into position in the mold. Mark where the cross struts have to be cut to permit the sides to drop flush to the sound board. Cut off the strut ends and make sure the sides will drop down properly. Remove the sides, leaving the sound board in the mold face down. Position the neck with the recessed table over the sound board where it will glue. With the neck perfectly aligned with the cen-

ter line of the mold, glue the neck to the sound board. Use a clamp at the heel and one along the neck to keep the neck flat against the mold. When dry, carefully fit the sides to the neck with the sides resting squarely along the entire perimeter of the sound board. Glue the sides to the neck, making sure the sides are not splayed.

Cut a strip of basswood 1/2" × 5/8" × 30". Slice this strip into 1/4" blocks. Lay each block flat and set a 1" chisel on their diagonal axis. A smart blow with a mallet will sever the blocks into two right-angle triangles. These individual blocks are glued at the corner where sides and top meet.

Place the corner blocks so they butt on each side of the two cross struts and approximately 1/8" apart from each other. Each block has to be sanded to conform to the curve where it will glue.

Brush Titebond or hide glue on the back and bottom of the glue blocks and set them in place. If Titebond is used, hold them in place for about 30 seconds. With hide glue, apply the glue, press the block home, and then lift it free. Wait a minute for the glue to get tacky and then press the block back in place.

The continuous bottom lining is fitted and glued in the regular way; so is the back. The mold itself is made into a gluing form by placing screws about the perimeter in the same way they are placed about the work board.

This method of assembly has the advantage of easily and accurately joining neck to top. Also, the mold is a more convenient device for holding the guitar while work proceeds than the work board. The work board is not needed.

The disadvantages are that one is restricted more or less to the shape of the mold. Moreover, the sides must fit into the mold without any forcing. And cutting, fitting, and gluing the many individual blocks is a more tedious process than gluing a kerfed lining.

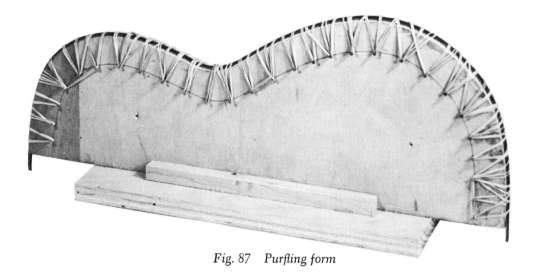

Fig. 87 Purfling form

Purfling

Purfling consists of alternating strips of dark and light veneers glued together to form a laminated member shaped to the contour of the guitar. Their purpose is to protect the leading edges of the guitar and seal off the end grain of the top and back.

The band-sawed sections of the original sandwich that were put aside must now be made into two purfling forms. One would suffice, but two permit work to continue on one form while the other is drying.

In all likelihood there will be a discrepancy in the original mold shape and the actual shape of the completed guitar. The purfling form must be altered to conform exactly to the final outline. Trace the guitar outline onto each section. Saw and sand each section to this corrected contour.

Pencil a line one inch from the contoured edge on both sides of each form. Nail ¾″ #17 nails along each line at one-inch intervals, leaving half of each nail protruding.

Cut two lengths of wood approximately 1″ × 4″ × 13″. Also cut four lengths of 1″ × 1″ × 8″ supports. Glue the forms along the center line of each base. Apply glue to the supports and nail them along the base angle of each form. Both forms are now ready for use.

The purfling for the top is usually wider and more elaborate than the purfling for the back. Fig. 88 shows a breakdown of purfling for top and back. Included is a fillet of black and white that goes around the side of the guitar. This purfling arrangement is suitable for both rosewood and maple guitars.

Clamp the form to a workbench and cover the contoured edge with plastic tape to keep the veneers from gluing to the form. Three dozen 3½″ rubber bands are needed for lacing the laminations tight against the form.

Laminations are assembled from the inside out. Lay the first strip of black-white-black on the form. Temporarily secure this to the form with a rubber band a few inches each side of the waist curve. Apply a layer of white glue to the waist and lay on the next strip—white-

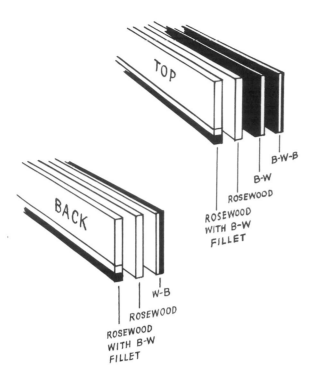

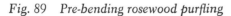

Fig. 88   *Purfling for top and back*

Fig. 89   *Pre-bending rosewood purfling*

black. Press both strips down against the form and wipe away excess glue with a damp cloth. Bind this glued section snugly against the form with some rubber bands, lacing them back and forth between nails until they are stretched taut. Guard against shifting the strips. They must glue together in perfect alignment. Remove the temporary rubber bands and apply glue to five-inch sections at a time, working out from the waist. Clean off excess glue and lace each section before proceeding to the next section. The purfling should protrude below the end of the lower bout. Bind this loose end by wrapping a rubber band around it several times and then back to the nails.

Move to the other form and repeat this procedure. By the time this form has been laced the first form will be dry. Remove the rubber bands from the first form. The next two layers are both rosewood strips. To prevent breaking at the waist these strips should be pre-bent at the waist. Boil some water in a small pot and loop the rosewood strip into it where the waist will fall. Pre-bend eight rosewood strips. If Fig. 88 is being followed, four of these strips will have to be the narrower width necessary to accommodate the black-white fillet. If the fillet is omitted, all eight strips will be the same width.

Another simple method for putting a bend in the rosewood purfling is to wedge some copper or brass tubing over the end of a soldering iron and clamp the handle in a vise. Press the strips against the hot tubing. Slide them back and forth against the hot surface until they are bent, a matter of a few seconds.

Two rosewood strips can be glued to the laminations on the form if the fillet is omitted. If the fillet is used it is best to glue the two final members separately. Glue the first rosewood strip in position on both forms.

In gluing the final strip with fillet, glue must be pressed up through the rosewood and fillet

Fig. 90   Cutting top purfling ledge

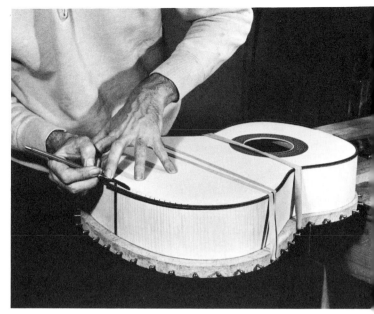

Fig. 91   Fitting purfling

while both strips are being glued down. Apply glue to a section and spread the strips. Bring them together so that glue is forced up through the joint. Gluing of these final strips with fillet must be done in reverse. The fillet strip will be on different sides on each form. This is very important. Inadvertent gluing of the fillets in the same place on each form will result in two purfling members for the same edge.

This completes the fabrication of the purfling for the top. Make the purfling for the back, following the same procedure. All will go smoothly if these cautions are studiously observed: Wipe away excess glue and keep the sides of each member perfectly square.

Before cutting the edge recess to lay in the purfling, the top and back plates must be smoothed to a uniform thickness all around the guitar perimeter. This final thickness will vary between $\frac{5}{64}$" and $\frac{3}{32}$".

Adjust the purfling cutter to cut a groove slightly smaller than the purfling. Test the width of cut on a scrap board. Lay the purfling against the cut to make sure the cut is smaller. With the cutter knife protruding about $\frac{3}{32}$" make the first incision around the top perimeter. Clamping the guitar to the work board will hold the guitar while the cutting proceeds. Make the first cuts with light pressure, increasing pressure as the incision becomes more pronounced and less likely to throw the knife. Repeat the cutting process until the bottom of the purfling cutter is resting on the sound board.

Stand the guitar on edge and cut the sides, stopping short of the bottom inlay. Hold the tool firmly with one hand and the guitar with the other. Keep the knife razor sharp.

The purfling recess must be continued into the neck area to conceal the ends of the purfling (Fig. 93). Cut these extensions with a narrow chisel.

Fig. 92 *Mitering plan for bottom inlay*

Cut through the sides until the corner comes away. Smooth the wall of the recess with a small piece of sandpaper folded in half. Hold it firmly against the wall and run it around the edge until the wall is a smooth contour. True the floor of the recess with a safe-edge file. The entire recess must be square.

Fit the purfling members into place (Fig. 91). Begin by clamping the guitar at the neck to the work board. Fit the waist first and secure it with a rubber band. Fitting proceeds from that point out to the ends. Secure with rubber bands as the fitting goes along.

Cut off the top end of the purfling to fit into the chiseled groove. Fit the bottom end of the purfling so that the fillet miters into the bottom inlay (Fig. 92). Check along the length of the fitted purfling for gaps. A smooth tight fit is essential before gluing. Both top strips may be glued simultaneously, but it is best for the novice guitar-maker to glue them separately the first time.

Coat the recess with hide or plastic resin glue and press in the purfling strip. Apply rubber bands, removing squeezed-out glue with a

damp cloth as work proceeds. Cover every visible inch of the purfling with a tight rubber band. Dry overnight.

Follow the same procedure on the back. File the heel down level with the bottom of the recess and butt the ends of the purfling. Hold these ends in place during gluing by driving two small finishing nails into the heel. Place them close enough to the purfling to wedge it up against the wall of the recess.

Later a piece of ebony salvaged from the waste portion of the fret board will be cut to the shape of the heel and glued in place.

Fig. 93 *Purfling ends finished off*

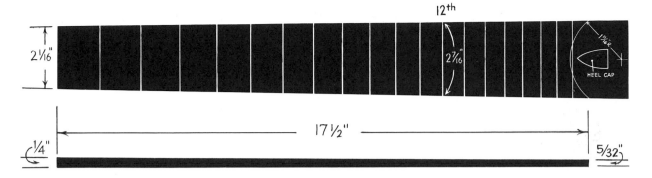

Fig. 94   Fret board diagram

Fret Board

Drill a small hole in each corner of the fret board and fasten it to a larger work board with a small finishing nail in each hole. Drive the nails well below the surface with a nail set.

Smooth this side of the fret board dead level, using scrapers and sanding stick. When a metal straightedge indicates that the surface is perfectly flat, remove the nails and turn the board over. Replace the nails, driving them in again below the surface.

Scrape and smooth the top to the bevel shown in Fig. 94.

Fret positions are laid out according to a traditional formula called the Rule of the Eighteenth. The vibrating string length is divided by 18 to locate the first fret. The remaining string length is again divided by 18 to find the second fret, and so on. This formula contains a slight error because 18 is only an approximate figure. A careful computation of actual frequency ratios of whole notes reveals a constant that is not exactly $\frac{1}{18}$th. The scale on page 72 is worked out according to this more precise formula.

Mark the fret grooves with a knife or pointed metal scriber against the edge of a try square.

Saw the slots to a depth of $\frac{1}{16}$" full with the medium back saw. Work the saw against the edge of the try square (Fig. 95) until the saw is well into the wood. A strip of masking tape on the side of the saw blade will help gauge the depth of cut.

Pencil a line down the center of the fret board, continuing onto the work board. Locate the axis for scribing the $3\frac{3}{8}$" circle that breaks through the nineteenth fret. Scribe the circle with dividers or compass. Draw the tapered sidelines on the fret board.

Remove the fret board and jigsaw the tapered side pieces and bottom arch. Sand the edges of the fret board smooth by running them over sandpaper.

Position the fret board on the neck so that the twelfth fret falls over the joint between neck and body. At the top of the fret board there should be a $\frac{5}{32}$" space for a bone or ivory nut.

Sand the neck with a sand block until it is level from top to sound hole. Check with a straightedge as work progresses. Rest the fret board in place and peer along the crack between fret board and neck. If light is observable through the crack, more leveling will be required. It is important that the fret board make

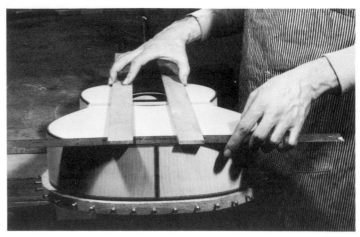

Fig. 95 *Cutting frets*   Fig. 96 *Aligning fret board*

Distances to Frets Taken from the Nut
(Based on a string length of $25^{21}/_{32}$″)

Frets	Inches nearest $^1/_{64}$″	Inches nearest 1/10,000″
1st	$1^7/_{16}$″	1.4329
2nd	$2^{51}/_{64}$″	2.7943
3rd	$4^5/_{64}$″	4.0769
4th	$5^{19}/_{64}$″	5.2918
5th	$6^7/_{16}$″	6.4302
6th	$7^{33}/_{64}$″	7.5107
7th	$8^{17}/_{32}$″	8.5257
8th	$9^{31}/_{64}$″	9.4913
9th	$10^{25}/_{64}$″	10.3982
10th	$11^1/_4$″	11.2557
11th	$12^1/_{16}$″	12.0636
12th	$12^{53}/_{64}$″	12.8262
13th	$13^{35}/_{64}$″	13.5447
14th	$14^7/_{32}$″	14.2254
15th	$14^{55}/_{64}$″	14.8667
16th	$15^{15}/_{32}$″	15.4731
17th	$16^3/_{64}$″	16.0434
18th	$16^{37}/_{64}$″	16.5836
19th	$17^3/_{32}$″	17.0926

contact with the neck and body of the guitar at all points without pressure.

Fasten the guitar to the work board with rubber bands and clamp the fret board lightly in position on the neck. Check the alignment of the fret board by placing two flat sticks or straightedges along each side of the fret board (Fig. 96). They should extend the length of the fret board down past the bottom of the guitar. If the fret board is properly aligned, the inner edges of the sticks will be equidistant from the center line at the bottom of the guitar. Position masking tape along each side of the fret board where it passes over the body to mark its centered position.

Clean the bottom of the fret board with a benzol-soaked rag. Apply hide glue to the fret board and to the area it will occupy on the guitar. Wait until both pieces are tacky—10 or 15 minutes—and then join them. Clamp the fret board (Fig. 97) and leave overnight.

The neck and heel must now be shaped to their final form. Glue on the heel cap.

Use the ½″ gouge to trim the heel flush with the fret board. Shape the neck to a flattened oval (Fig. 103) with rasp and sanding sticks. Finish the sanding with fine sandpaper.

Cut nineteen lengths of fret wire with a wire clipper. Each fret wire should be about ½″ longer than the groove in which it will lie.

Fasten the guitar to the work board with rubber bands and support the neck with a block of wood and a rubber cushion to protect the neck.

Mix a small quantity of epoxy cement and work some into each groove with a thin strip of veneer or a knife.

Move the support directly under the first fret and lay the fret wire in place with an equal overhang on each end. Hold the fret wire in place with one hand and hammer in the tang with the other hand. Remove hand and finish hammering in the fret wire. Tap the overhang on each end to crimp over slightly and insure a tight fit of the fret wire at the edges.

Move the support and repeat this operation until the ninth fret. From the tenth to fourteenth frets the heel and foot of the neck provide enough support. The last five frets should be hammered in with a support held or positioned inside the body to receive some of the force of the hammer blows—a precaution to prevent knocking loose a side bracket.

The nineteenth fret requires two pieces of fret wire. Do not allow for any overhang on the inside edge of this fret.

Wipe away all forced-out cement as the work progresses. Allow the fret board to dry overnight.

Clip off all the overhangs with a pair of wire nippers and file the ends flush with the fret board. Use a sheet of tin to protect the sound board while filing the twelfth to nineteenth frets. File an oblique face on the end of each fret wire with a small metal file. Take care to keep from gouging the edge of the fret board with the file.

Rest a steel straightedge on the frets to see if they are level. If not, slide a carborundum stone (the longer the better) or a flat file over the tops of the frets until level. Sight down from the head along each edge and top of the frets for irregularities. Buff the frets with a piece of crocus cloth. If staining is necessary dip some stain (*Ebonholzbeize*) onto a cotton swab or small artist's brush and coat the light streaks. Wait until dry and polish with a dry cloth to remove any unabsorbed residue.

Remove the masking tape alongside the lower portion of the fret board and remove any trace of adhesive with benzol.

Fig. 97 Clamping fret board to neck

Fig. 98 Clamping ebony heel cap

Fig. 99 *Hammering in frets over neck support*

Fig. 100 Filing fret ends

Fig. 101 Leveling frets with carborundum stone

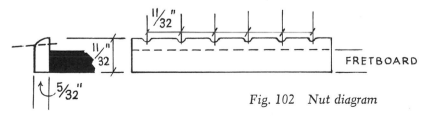

Fig. 102 Nut diagram

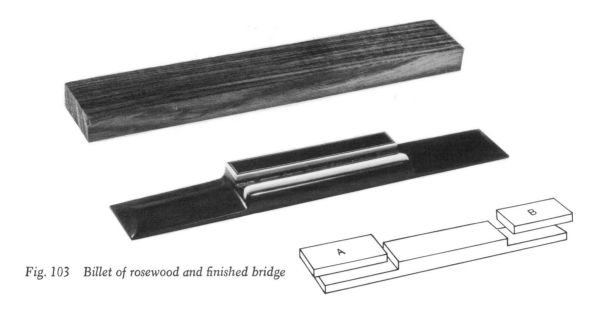

Fig. 103   *Billet of rosewood and finished bridge*

Bridge

Besides being an important link in the transmission of string vibrations to the diaphragm, the bridge also affords an opportunity for artistic embellishment.

The most popular bridge design incorporates a strip of bone or ivory on the leading edges of the rectangular block where the string ends are secured. A pleasing variation uses bone or ivory on all four sides of the rectangle with a thin white inline. Torres used a thin sheet of ivory to cover the entire face of the rectangle. All these designs have the basic function of preventing grooves in the rosewood caused by the strain of taut nylon strings.

As a rule the arms of the bridge are left unadorned, finished with an oblique facet on each end. Sometimes a small dot of ivory or mother-of-pearl is inlaid in the center of each arm. Some luthiers are wary of using mother-of-pearl on guitars, believing that it has a tone-deadening effect. Ivory, curiously enough, is considered safe for inlay.

Mark the saw lines on the sides and top of a rosewood billet and saw out the two large sections A and B (above). Affix the rough bridge to a larger work board with tacks alongside the arms. Clamp this work board to the workbench and saw out the valley and the saddle groove. Clean up the valley with a small gouge or folded piece of sandpaper so that the strings will slide readily up the rise to the saddle when they come through the hole. If the incline from the saddle down to the base of the rectangular tie block makes too sharp an angle the string ends will have to be fished out with long-nosed pliers, a bothersome chore.

Cut the corner recesses for the bone inlay. Clean and true them with a small safe-edge file. Clamp a 1/16"-thick sheet of bone or ivory upright in a vise. Saw through it with a coping saw, using a very fine blade. Because bone and ivory are fairly brittle it is wise to saw carefully and hold the sheet near the point where the blade is sawing. Saw halfway down and then reverse the sheet. Saw from the other end to meet your first cut.

Cut the pieces slightly oversize and true the gluing edges. Glue them in place with epoxy.

Clamp a wooden caul with waxed paper over the top of the tie block. This will keep the inlay from rising when C clamps are applied for horizontal pressure (Fig. 111).

To make the inlay with inline that frames all four sides of the tie block, three glued up strips must be prepared—one each for the long edges and one to be sawed in half for the small end edges.

Saw three thin strips of bone or ivory and glue black-white purfling to a smoothed edge on each strip. Cut a recess on all four sides of the tie block. Fit the inlay with mitered corners like a frame. Glue the long strips first and wait until they are glued before fitting the end pieces. When gluing is completed, sand the top of the tie block flush.

The arms are rounded with file and sanding sticks. A thin 1/32″ edge is left all around the arms. Do not sand them to a knife edge.

Mark the spaces for the holes and clamp the bridge in a drill-press vise adjusted to the proper angle. Drill the holes with a 1/16″ drill.

Bridges for flamenco guitars are much lower than classic-guitar bridges to bring the strings down closer to the sound board. This closer distance permits tapping (*golpe*) with greater ease, an important feature of flamenco playing. To permit lowering the tie block, the valley is undercut where it meets the arms (Fig. 114).

The saddle must sit squarely and firmly in its groove. A thin file with a flat milled edge is used to true the saddle groove. The bone or ivory saddle is left untrimmed in height until the fret board is glued on with frets in place.

Fig. 104   Sawing out valley

Fig. 105   Shaping bridge arms

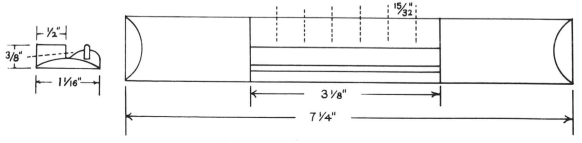

Fig. 106   Bridge diagram

Fig. 107   Bridge with 1/16" ivory strips on both edges of tie block

Fig. 108   Top of tie block covered with thin sheet of ivory

Fig. 109   Drilling string holes

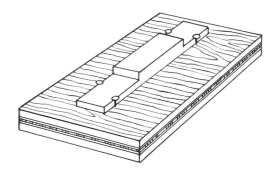

Fig. 110   Bridge work board

Fig. 111   Clamping ivory trim

Gluing the Bridge

Position the bridge so that the saddle stops the string exactly $12^{29}\!/_{32}''$ from the twelfth fret. Theoretically, the twelfth fret lies midway between nut and saddle; the harmonic octave at the twelfth fret should respond in the same pitch as fingered notes at the twelfth fret. In actual practice this will not occur unless the bridge is moved back an additional $^5\!/_{64}''$ because of the increased string tension caused by fingering. Lengthening the string compensates for the increased tension.

Make sure the bridge is perfectly aligned and centered. Mark its position lightly with a sharp pencil. Clean the entire bridge with benzol and coat the top surfaces with a wash coat of shellac reduced to 1 part white shellac to 5 parts alcohol by volume. The bridge must be filled and sealed (see section on finishing, page 86) before it is glued in place. This is necessary to eliminate the possibility of the rosewood "bleeding" onto the sound board if it is finished after gluing.

Glue the bridge in place with plastic resin glue. If the bridge is slightly arched and hugs the surface of the sound board, it can be clamped with one clamp (Fig. 112). Otherwise the clamping arrangement shown in Fig. 113 may be used.

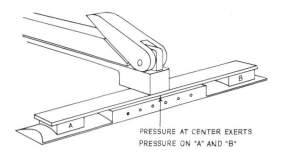

PRESSURE AT CENTER EXERTS
PRESSURE ON "A" AND "B"

Fig. 112   Clamping with fitted cauls

Fig. 113   Clamping with three clamps

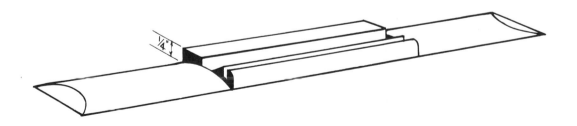

Fig. 114   Flamenco bridge

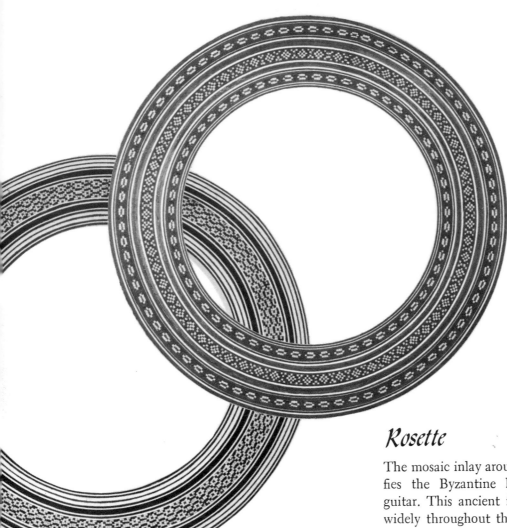

Rosette

The mosaic inlay around the sound hole identifies the Byzantine heritage of the Spanish guitar. This ancient form of marquetry—used widely throughout the Middle East—persisted through the centuries when the sound holes of European guitars and lutes were adorned with the Romanesque–Gothic tracery of the pierced and carved rose.

The complex appearance of the mosaic inlay belies the ease with which they can be made. A simple rosette can be made in a few hours. Complex rosettes may take as long as eight to ten hours to make.

Mosaic inlays are made of a series of tiles sliced from a mosaic log. This log consists of a number of planks made of thin, square wooden sticks of different colors arranged to form a design.

Wooden strips for making rosettes are available $\frac{1}{32}''$ square and come in different colors: white, straw, black, red, blue, green; brown (rosewood) strips $\frac{1}{32}''$ square are too fragile to work with. The others are easy to work with and, despite their seeming fragility, present no real problems in handling. For those afraid of working with such a narrow gauge, strips are obtainable $\frac{1}{16}''$ square.

Designs are sketched on graph paper with colored pencils. Fig. 116 shows a simple design broken down into a working drawing.

Cut the necessary number of sticks of each color to 8″ lengths. Separate them into groups representing each plank in the log.

Fasten a sheet of waxed paper to a flat working surface under a good strong light. Assemble each plank in proper sequence. Lay the sticks comprising the first plank alongside one another and put a strip of masking tape over one end to hold them together on the waxed paper. Do the same with each plank.

Using an artist's brush, apply hide glue to the waxed paper beneath the first plank. To do this the loose end of the plank has to be lifted clear of the paper. Leave the taped end anchored. Before setting the plank down onto the glue, fan out the sticks. Lay them down in this position and then squeeze them together, forcing glue up between them. Remove the tape and force glue up through this end of the plank. When each stick is stuck to its neighbor, lift the plank to a clear space on the waxed paper. Hold down one end and gently wipe excess glue from both sides of the plank with a moist cloth. Now check the plank against a straightedge to make sure it is not crooked. Let it dry while proceeding with other planks in the same manner.

When all the planks are dry (1 hour) scrape their flat sides gently with a razor to even out any discrepancies in size. Stack the planks one on the other and examine the end. Make sure the end pattern matches your design. Spread a thin layer of hide glue between the planks and glue them together. Press them together with your fingers; clamping is not necessary. When the log is thoroughly dry, cut off three tiles.

Tiles cut from a perfectly square log will not work around a circle. The tiled segments have to be tapered to butt against each other around a curve. Carefully trim both sides of the log to a uniform taper by scraping with a razor blade or a sand block. The log is now complete and can be sliced like a loaf of bread into tiles. Slicing the log into $\frac{1}{16}''$ tiles, however, is tricky. A small miter box must be built to fit the log. Saw a slot at one end of the miter box. Glue in a small stop at a point just past the slot that will make each tile the same thickness. If the log is not immobilized during sawing there is danger of dislodging bits of the tile.

The form for assembling the rosette consists of a block of wood about 8″ × 12″ and a $3\frac{9}{16}''$ circle cut from $\frac{1}{8}''$ Masonite. Waxed paper (the kind sold for freezer use is best) is wrapped about the block and taped at the edges. Two small holes have been drilled through the Masonite circle to allow it to be fastened to the middle of the block with two nails. Additional items required are one dozen push pins, tweezers, a small brush for applying hide glue, and a cup of water.

Fig. 115 Carved rose of lute
(Max Unverdorben, sixteenth-century)

Fig. 116   Simple mosaic design

Fig. 117   Cross-section of log

Fig. 118   Gluing up planks

Before commencing the actual assembly, prepare a working model of a small segment of the rosette. Glue the first three tiles together on white cardboard or a scrap of wood. Cut short pieces of banding and glue them on both sides of the tile section. Scrape the segment smooth so that the design is clear.

Wrap the first strip around the Masonite circle, keeping it tight. Overlap the ends and slice through them with a knife or razor so that they butt and lie snug against the circle. Apply a dab of glue to the joint and glue this initial joint to the circle itself to keep the strip from shifting. Place push pins next to the joint to hold it firmly in place. Apply glue to the entire side of the first strip and to the side of the second strip. Remove the push pins and lay the second strip tight around the first strip, using push pins around the perimeter to hold the strip in place. Join each strip in a different place. Allow the glue to set for a few minutes before laying in the strips. They will grab more securely and insure a tighter rosette. If one band is loose the rosette will come off the form out of round. For a good fit around the sound hole it is essential that the rosette be as round as possible.

Glue in strips until the mosaic portion is reached. Cut three tiles from the log. Lift each tile with the tweezers and dip it in and out of the cup of water. Smear some glue on the last strip and set the tiles in place against the strip. As each tile is positioned, brush some glue on the edges that butt. When the three are in place take the next strip and glue it to the outside of the tiles. This strip will serve as a retaining wall for the tiles as they are set in place. Stick push pins against this strip to hold the tiles against the inner strip. The water will have softened the glue holding the bits of mosaic together and permit squeezing the tiles into a tight fit. Use the tweezers as a prod, pushing and coaxing the tiles into an unbroken pattern.

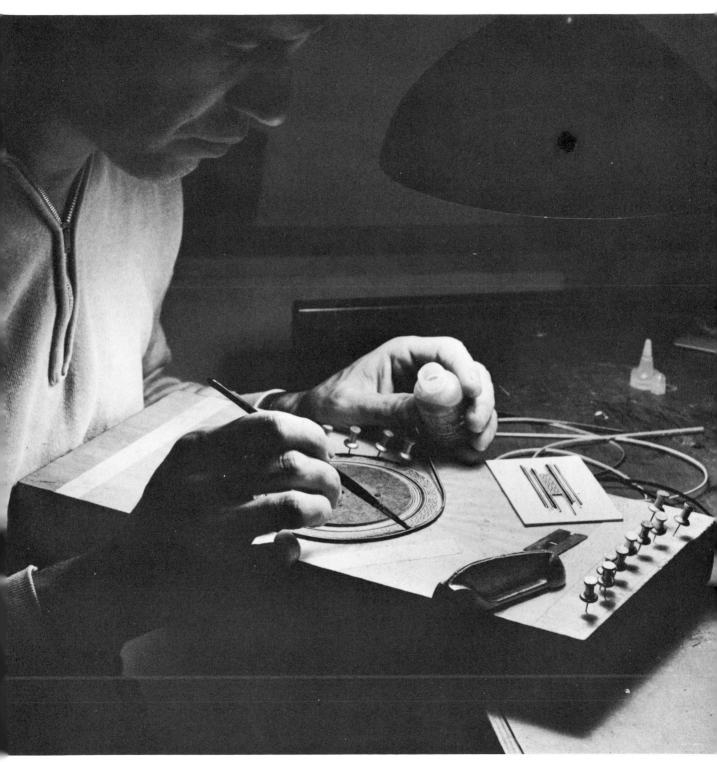

Fig. 119 *Gluing in tiles and strips*

Rosette   83

Fig. 120   Work board with sample section

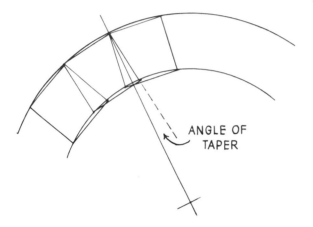

ANGLE OF
TAPER

Fig. 121   Method of calculating taper

Fig. 122   Miter box to hold log

It may happen that the tiles resist neat juxtaposition because of insufficient taper. Do not remove these tiles but let them dry in place.

Increase the taper of the log slightly by scraping again with the razor. Cut three more tiles, moisten, and glue them in place next to the first three. If they fit well continue around the circle keeping the retaining strip tight all the way. If not, further adjustment of the taper is necessary. The ill-fitting group of three can be concealed under the fret board when the rosette is inlaid.

Strips for the banding can be cut from purfling strips. At certain thicknesses some of these strips will crack under the strain of bending them into a tight circle. This can be avoided by soaking them in hot water until pliable enough to bend into a circle without breaking. Clamp the ends with a spring clothespin where they intersect and put them aside to dry. The longest strips needed for banding a rosette are about 19″ long. The fine strips used in manufactured purfling can be easily separated by soaking in hot water for fifteen minutes. Prebending these fine strips is unnecessary.

When the rosette is complete, lift the nails and free the Masonite circle. Sand the top of the rosette level. Cut the rosette loose from the waxed paper backing and sand away any paper stuck to the rosette. Store the rosette between two blocks of wood until ready to use.

An eight-inch log of average thickness sliced in one-sixteenths will make two rosettes.

Fig. 123   Hauser rosette

Fig. 124 *Final sanding*

Finishing

Sand the entire guitar carefully with #7/0 sandpaper; sand purfling edges to a gentle round. Varnish will adhere more successfully to a rounded edge than to a sharp one.

If the sound board has been brought down to the correct thickness it should respond in B or B *flat* when struck a light, glancing blow with the thumb. A study of guitars by the great makers reveals no consistent pattern in the tuning of plates, although it is known that an A tuning will sometimes give the open A string a strident fullness. Santos Hernandez is reported to have strung his guitars prior to finishing for final adjustment of the sound board. Relying on his ear, he strummed and then sanded, tapering the sound board gradually from the bridge to the outer edge until it sounded right.

Guitars, unlike violins, do not need eleven or fourteen coats of varnish. The layering of varnish or lacquer on a guitar can, in fact, hurt the tone. No more finish need be applied to a guitar than is necessary properly to seal and protect the surface. A good finish enhances the appearance of the guitar by accentuating the beauty of the wood. More important, however, is sealing off the wood to retard the absorption of atmospheric moisture and protect against normal wear and tear. Varnish seems to give guitars an added "brightness"; it also raises their pitch slightly.

Rub the top lightly with a damp cloth to raise the grain. When dry, sand it smooth again with fine finishing paper. Prepare rosewood for finishing by first cleaning the surface with a benzol-soaked rag. Tease out as much free oil as possible by rubbing until no more color comes off on the rag.

For best results finishing should be done in a workroom temperature of 75 to 80 degrees.

At all stages of finishing humidity is an adverse influence; finishing should be postponed if the relative humidity exceeds 60 per cent.

Open-pore woods such as rosewood and mahogany must be filled. Filler is a mixture of ground silex and color in a varnish-type vehicle and comes in several colors. The color of filler used should be a shade darker than the wood it will fill. Maple and spruce are close-grain woods and do not require filling.

Give the entire guitar (except fret board) a wash coat of 5-pound cut white shellac reduced five parts alcohol to one part shellac by volume. Shellac has a shelf life of six to eight months and must be fresh to dry properly. This preliminary wash coat makes the filling operation easier and gives cleaner results. It also stops color changes in the wood by retarding the absorption of oils and resins contained in filler. Allow at least an hour for drying before filling.

Dig a lump of filler out of the can and mix it with benzine (do not use benzol) until it has the consistency of paint. Brush it on parallel to the grain with an old paintbrush, working it into the pores. Avoid getting any filler onto the spruce sound board.

When the filler dries to a fogged or cloudy appearance—usually twenty minutes—wipe off the excess filler with a coarse cloth. Remove the excess by rubbing across the grain with enough pressure to pad and pack the filler more firmly into the pores. Finish wiping by rubbing parallel to the grain with a soft, lint-free cloth. If the filler is wiped before it is sufficiently dry it will be pulled from the pores. If the filler is too dry when wiped it will give muddy results. Practice and good judgment will yield a professional job.

Filling may have to be done twice to fill all the pores and provide a hard, smooth base for finishing. The final finish can be no better than the surface underneath.

Before any finish is applied to the guitar, the filler must be absolutely dry. Laying varnish or other coating on partially dry filler is a common finishing hazard. The final finish will not dry—necessitating removal of all finishing materials down to the wood and starting all over again. Allow at least a day, preferably two, for drying filler.

When dry, coat the guitar with shellac reduced one part shellac to two parts alcohol. For best results, allow this sealing coat to dry

Fig. 125 *Wire hanger for holding guitar during varnishing*

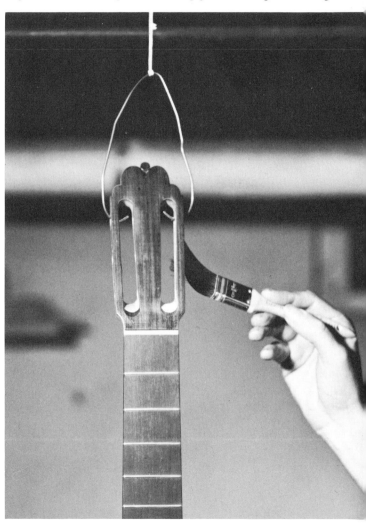

overnight before lightly sanding with #7/0 paper. When thoroughly dry, shellac will not adhere to sandpaper but will leave a fine, white powder on the surface. If the paper becomes gummed up either the shellac is inferior or humidity has slowed the normal drying action.

Sealing is essential on rosewood because rosewood will bleed under lacquer and will also seriously delay the drying of oil varnish. Use only one coat for sealing.

Both varnish and lacquer are used to finish guitars. Generally speaking, a good oil varnish will produce a more durable finish than will lacquer. Varnish is also easier to apply by brush; lacquer is usually applied by spray gun.

A good varnish for guitars is tough, flexible, and clear. Drying time should be at least a day. Quick-drying varnishes are not suitable for musical instruments. H. Behlen & Brothers (see page 95) market a lacquer—Qualatone #317—flexible enough for guitar finishing. In all cases, the manufacturer's recommendations for thinning and drying time must be followed.

Apply varnish with a soft-hair 1″ flagged-and-tipped brush. Twirl a new brush between your palms to shake out loose hairs. Do not use a varnish brush for anything but varnish.

Apply varnish in long, even strokes with a minimum of brushing. Varnish the sound board first. A clean, dry rag stuffed under the sound hole will keep varnish from dripping into the interior. Varnish the inner edge of the sound hole and the sides of the finger board. Work under a good light to make sure no spot is left unvarnished. Coat the purfling edges carefully. When the top is done, stand the guitar upright on some newspapers and varnish the sides. Supporting the neck with one hand, begin at the heel and apply varnish to the sides down to the lower bout. Using a suspended hook (Fig. 125) shaped from a coat hanger to hang the guitar, finish varnishing the bottom section of the sides. Hold the neck and varnish

the back. To steady the guitar while varnishing the head, neck, and heel, hook a forefinger through the sound hole in back of the fret board and press your thumb against the face of the fret board.

When the varnish is dry, sand lightly with fine sandpaper—varnish does not adhere well to a glossy surface. Apply three coats, sanding between each coat. Before applying the fourth and last coat, sand away all bumps caused by dripping and overlaps.

The varnish must dry for two weeks—the longer the better—before being rubbed to its final polished finish. A wise practice is to string the guitar and play it for a month before rubbing it down.

Varnish is smoothed with 400A wet-or-dry silicon carbide paper and water. Dip a folded piece of the paper into water and carefully sand away all lumps and unevenness. Inspect the surface frequently to avoid going through the finish. After initial smoothing has been accomplished, change to 600A silicon carbide paper and rub until all surface scratches are polished out. Be very careful when sanding the edges, the easiest place to go through the finish. This rubbing operation softens the varnish and final polishing must be delayed for another week. A special rubbing compound rubbed with a felt pad will give the surface a high polish. Powdered rottenstone and water will do the same job.

If lacquer is used, apply four or five coats. Brushing must be done quickly because lacquer dries rapidly. Sanding between coats is unnecessary. Final rubbing and polishing are the same as for varnish.

Groove the nut and string the guitar by fastening the 1 and 6 strings first, 2 and 5 next, and 3 and 4 last.

A new guitar's full tonal possibilities are not realized until it has been thoroughly "played in."

Hermann Hauser, 1949
(*classic*)

Body length ......18 5/8″
Upper bout ......10 15/32″
Waist .... 8 7/8″
Lower bout ......13 7/8″
Upper depth ..... 3 3/8″
Bottom depth .... 3 9/16″

Marcelo Barbero, 1955
(*flamenco*)

Body length ......19″
Upper bout ......11″
Waist .... 9 1/2″
Lower bout ......14 3/8″
Upper depth ..... 3 3/8″
Bottom depth .... 3 3/4″

Vicente Arias, 1870
(*classic*)

Body length ......18 1/4"
Upper bout ......10 3/16"
Waist .... 8 5/8"
Lower bout ......13 5/8"
Upper depth ..... 3 9/16"
Bottom depth .... 3 13/16"

Domingo Esteso, 1923
(*classic*)

Body length ......19 1/8"
Upper bout ......10 13/16"
Waist .... 9 3/16"
Lower bout ......14 3/16"
Upper depth ..... 3 11/16"
Bottom depth .... 3 7/8"

Vicente Arias, 1894
(*classic*)

Body length ......18 11/16"
Upper bout ......10 1/2"
Waist .... 8 5/8"
Lower bout ......13 7/8"
Upper depth ..... 3 3/8"
Bottom depth .... 3 5/8"

Santos Hernandez, 1932
(*flamenco*)

Body length ......19 3/16"
Upper bout ......10 13/16"
Waist .... 9 5/16"
Lower bout ......14 5/16"
Upper depth ..... 3 1/2"
Bottom depth .... 3 3/4"

SUPPLY SOURCES

H. L. Wild Co., 510 East Eleventh Street, New York, N. Y. Wood, tools, tuning machines and all guitar-making accessories. Catalog.

Vitali Import Co., 5944-48 Atlantic Blvd., Maywood, Calif. Wood, tuning machines and all guitar-making accessories. Catalog.

J. F. Wallo, 1319 "F" Street N.W., Washington, D.C. Wood, varnish and guitar-making accessories. Catalog.

Metropolitan Music Co., 222 Park Avenue South, New York, N. Y. Wood, pegs. Catalog.

H. Behlen & Bro. Inc., 10 Christopher Street, New York, N. Y. Everything used in wood finishing. Catalog.

BIBLIOGRAPHY

Alton, Robert. *Violin and 'Cello Building and Repairing*. London: Cassell, 1950.

Behlen, H., & Bro., Inc. *The Art of Wood Finishing*. New York: H. Behlen & Bro., Inc., 1957.

Helmholtz, Hermann. *The Sensations of Tone*. New York: Dover, 1954.

Hill, W. Henry. *Antonio Stradivari*. New York: Dover, 1963.

Hofmeister, Theodorus, Jr. "Torres, the Creator of the Modern Guitar." *Guitar Review*,* No. 16 (1954).

Huttig, H. E., II. "The Guitar Maker and His Techniques." *Guitar Review*, No. 28 (1965).

Muñoz, Richard. *Technology of the Argentina Guitar* (trans. Dr. E. H. Taves). Buenos Aires, Argentina, 1952.

Wood Handbook, U. S. Department of Agriculture, U. S. Government Printing Office, Washington, D.C., 20402.

* *Guitar Review* is published by the Society of the Classic Guitar, 409 East 50th Street, New York, N. Y. It is a handsome magazine devoted to all aspects of the classic guitar.